THE FORGOTTEN TREASURE OF INDULGENCES

L. S. SCARPITTA, M.A.

MULTI-SERVICES PUBLISHING COMPANY

The Forgotten Treasure of Indulgences
Since Vatican II

or

INDULGENCES:
WHAT THEY ARE AND HOW TO GET THEM

By L. S. Scarpitta, M.A.

*Help for the Forgiveness of the Punishment Due to Sin
For Ourselves and For The Souls in Purgatory*

TABLE OF CONTENTS

PART TWO
QUESTIONS AND ANSWERS

EPIGRAPH

"An indulgence, which the Church grants to the penitent, is a manifestation of the marvelous Communion of Saints, which by the single bond of charity of Christ mystically unites the Most Blessed Virgin Mary and the company of the faithful, whether triumphant in Heaven or detained in Purgatory or still living as pilgrims upon earth. For an indulgence, given by the intervention of the Church, lessens or entirely remits the punishment, by which a person is in a certain sense prevented from obtaining closer union with God. The repentant, therefore, will find in this unique form of ecclesial charity an ever-available help..."

Epistle Sacrosancta Portiunculae
Pope Paul VI (1966)

INTRODUCTION

Author's Personal Introduction To The Book

Prior to relocating some years ago, indulgences had been one of several Church-related topics on which I had repeatedly been asked to speak at a number of parishes in three Southern California archdioceses.

This book was originally begun to provide support and reference material for a group whose goal would have been to offer prayers and assistance for the Souls in Purgatory. There are religious orders and groups in the Church for which prayers for the Poor Souls are especially important.

Since June of 1981, it has been reported that Our Lady has been appearing in the village of Medjugorje in Bosnia-Hercegovina. Many messages have been coming from Medjugorje, primarily emphasizing peace, faith, conversion, penance, fasting, and especially an urgent call to frequent prayer.

In a special Note in September 2024, signed by Pope Francis, the Catholic Church gave its approval to effectively all of the many messages which have come from there. A request for prayers for the Souls in Purgatory have been mentioned in the messages on more than one occasion.

For example, on July 21, 1982, the following message came from Medjugorje:

> *"There are a large number of souls who have been in Purgatory*
> *for a long time because no one prays for them."*

That same day, a strong message was given regarding the power of prayer and fasting. *"... Through fasting and prayer, one can stop wars, one can suspend the laws of nature..."* It appears to be true that people have indeed forgotten the importance and power of prayer.

On January 10, 1983, part of a message from Medjugorje said:

> *"... It is not on All Souls Day, but at Christmas, that the greatest number of souls leave Purgatory. There are in Purgatory, souls who pray ardently to God, but for whom no relative or friend prays for them on earth. God makes them benefit from the prayers of other people. It happens that God permits them to manifest themselves in different ways, close to their relatives on earth, in order to remind men of the existence of Purgatory, and to solicit their prayers close to God who is just, but good."*

On November 6, 1986:

> *"Dear children, today I invite you to pray every day for the Souls in Purgatory. Every soul needs prayer and grace in order to reach God and His love. By this way, dear children, you will gain new intercessors, who will help you during your life to discern that nothing on earth is more important for you than longing for heaven.*

> *"For that, dear children, pray without respite so that you may be able to help yourselves and others for whom your prayers will bring joy."*

Although the Souls in Purgatory will eventually get to Heaven even without our prayers, their suffering can be greatly shortened by our prayers.

In December of 1983, several spiritual cautions were given, as well as strong support for the importance of monthly confession:

> *"There are many Christians, who are no longer faithful, because they do not pray anymore... Monthly confession will be a remedy for the Church in the West. Whole sections of the church could be cured, if the believers would go to confession once a month."*

Confession is a critical part of the indulgence process.

The current structure of indulgences within the Catholic Church truly is an aid in leading a more powerful spiritual life. The current regulations support a disposition of spiritual awareness and strength.

The requirements for obtaining plenary indulgences, especially, foster frequent reception of both the Sacrament of Penance and also communion, an ongoing awareness of conscience and of our spiritual shortcomings and strengths, and a deeper understanding of the closeness and love of God.

Among some theologians and clergy today, disputes exist regarding certain aspects of the interpretation of the Church's teaching on indulgences. This book does not wish to interfere with productive discussions of this topic.

However, there are also people who appear to condescendingly support indulgences while at the same time making it plain that they themselves do not use them. Some of these people seem to be saying, *"Isn't that cute, they're still using indulgences..."*

It is also clear that some people would prefer that the Church discontinue all mention of indulgences. Without directly attacking the Church's position, they seem to find it necessary to call into question everything possible concerning this doctrine and anything else of which they personally disapprove.

Although there are indeed areas in the Church which are in need of improvement, public disapproval of an actual Church doctrine can lead to an unneeded questioning of other judgments or teachings of the Church.

Regarding indulgences, there are those, even among the clergy, who make clear their non-acceptance, even personal disdain, for this teaching.

It is the author's opinion that such attitudes are not only unproductive, but potentially damaging to the faithful and thus to the Church itself. It would appear that such attitudes indicate a failure to actually understand the purpose and very real benefits gained through the current structure of indulgences in the Catholic Church today. Additionally, the author questions such people's understanding as to what prayer, faith, and love really are — as well as what we can accomplish through the practice of the Divine Mercy — and through our love of God.

The faithful do not benefit from those who downplay the benefits and help available through this treasury of merits and grace within the Church. The benefits of frequent reception of the sacraments, the awareness of sin, the importance of the saints, of Daily Mass, and of certain devotions, as well as the importance of prayerful fasting and penance for our sins — including an awareness and use of indulgences — have been too long ignored in favor of supposedly more "enlightened" spiritual pursuits.

Such "enlightened" pursuits have led to a morally naïve world, to a world which has forgotten that God, in His great power, is no less in charge today than he has been throughout the history of the world. God has never been happy with sinners. Nor has He been particularly pleased with people who, by their indifference, pay little or no attention to Him.

Some of today's non-Catholic Christians seem to have a feeling that since Jesus came and died for our sins, and since God is so merciful, we can pretty much do what we want since our sins are all taken care of.

For those people, there is some bad news: Hell still exists. And people who commit serious sin still go there.

The knowledge and use of Church indulgences may not be critical to our salvation, but people today can use every bit of spiritual help they can get. Indulgences are one of the helps, given by the Church, which can assist us in growing a more unselfish love, a stronger spirituality, and an awareness of our own mortality, as well as the ongoing presence of God.

PREFACE

This book was written to explain the changes in indulgences in the Catholic Church since the late 1960s, and to answer some common questions and concerns. It is not meant to replace the current document, the *Manual of Indulgences, Fourth Edition (5th printing: 2017),* used by this book, the reading of which is strongly encouraged, especially by the clergy and hierarchy.

> *Note that although the Manual was translated into English from the fourth edition in 1999, evidence that it was updated since 1999 is clear both by its later inclusion of the section on Divine Mercy, and by also noting that its first printing was in October 2006.*

Because indulgences long ago fell into disuse by so many, their proper and prayerful use must again be taught and promoted. However, the value of the *Manual of Indulgences* extends beyond the indulgences themselves.

You will note some repetition in this book. That is sometimes done so as to clarify or emphasize certain concepts and requirements. There is repetition even in the *Manual* itself.

This book is based on the 4th edition of the *Manual of Indulgences*. Should a new edition be released, be sure to refer to the newest one for the Church's authentic collection of prayers and works, as well as for any changes to the regulations.

The *Enchiridion of Indulgences*[1] was first published after Vatican II in 1968. The English edition was published the following year. Its name was eventually changed to the *Manual of Indulgences*. It has been revised several times. As does the *Manual* now, the earlier *Enchiridion of Indulgences* provided the official Church teaching on indulgences in its time.

The *Forgotten Treasure of Indulgences* tries to provide a more straightforward summary of indulgences and their current regulations, while periodically adding some examples and analogies.

The complete and authentic collection of prayers and pious works to which the Apostolic See has attached indulgences is found in the *Manual of Indulgences* itself. By way of example, this book presents only samples of what is found in that more complete collection.

The *Manual of Indulgences, 4th Edition,* contains an abundance of additional information, discussion, and references. The current authorized English edition is only about 160 pages long, including its important appendices and indices. It is not particularly difficult to read.

All priests, religious, and the hierarchy itself should read the full *Manual of Indulgences* to understand what the

---

1. The word "Enchiridion" means a handbook or a manual. The word itself is derived from a Greek word meaning "in hand."

Church is telling us. Lay Catholics who would like a fuller discussion of the Church's current regulations on indulgences beyond what is in this book are also encouraged to read it.

The *Manual of Indulgences* is invaluable in providing the complete listing of indulgenced prayers and pious works — although additional indulgences (sometimes just for a single time or event) are periodically given by the Church.

The *Manual of Indulgences* is quoted frequently throughout this book, especially in places where the Church's exact meaning is important so as to accurately understand a topic. Quoted sentences or phrases that are not referenced in the main body of the book are taken from the *Manual of Indulgences*.

PART ONE

THE FORGOTTEN TREASURE OF INDULGENCES SINCE VATICAN II

CHAPTER 1
INDULGENCES: WHAT ARE THEY?

Indulgences Defined

> *An indulgence is a remission before God of the temporal punishment for sins, whose guilt is forgiven, which a properly disposed member of the Christian faithful obtains under certain and clearly defined conditions through the intervention of the Church, which, as the minister of Redemption, dispenses and applies authoritatively the treasury of the expiatory works of Christ and the saints.*

—from the *Manual of Indulgences (4th ed)*

∼

Through the Sacrament of Penance (confession), sins may be forgiven. But such forgiveness, by itself, may not erase the punishment due for those sins.

A PARTIAL indulgence frees a person from part of the punishment due to sins which have been forgiven. A

PLENARY indulgence frees a person from all of the punishment due to sins which have already been forgiven.

The main concern of the Church has been to attach greater importance to leading a Christian life, rather than just repeating various formulas and actions. With a right frame of mind and intent, indulgences can help in that.

∾

What Indulgences Are *Not* For

Indulgences are for one thing only: the reduction or elimination of punishment due to our forgiven sins. They can only be applied to ourselves or to the dead (the suffering Souls in Purgatory). They may not be applied to other living people.

Indulgences have nothing to do with any other intention. For example, the Church's regulations on indulgences have nothing to do with our prayers for things such as:

The conversion of sinners;
Intentions of Jesus or Mary, other than for the Souls in Purgatory and penance for our own sins:
The Pope's intentions and protection;
Vocations;
Faith;
Peace in ourselves or in the world;
Our individual needs and intentions.

It is important to pray often for those and for many other intentions.

However:

(1) Prayers for the Souls in Purgatory and,

(2) Prayers for the remission of punishment due to our own forgiven sins are the only two intentions — although very important and often neglected ones — to which indulgences apply.

It is through the dispensing of indulgences that the Church shows its concern not only for our own possible suffering in the life to come, but also for the suffering of those who have already died.

The Church's application of *"the treasury of the expiatory works of Christ and the saints"* should foster in us a constant awareness of the seriousness of sin and of the punishment due, even though those sins — and those of the Souls in Purgatory — may have already been forgiven.

Indulgences increase the good which we can obtain anyway through our good works and actions. Therefore, even without the benefit of indulgences, our good works, prayers, and actions obtain important graces for us and may also lead to a reduction of the temporal punishment due to our sins.

The benefits of indulgences can be applied to punishment that we ourselves may have to endure in Purgatory as we prepare ourselves to eventually enter Heaven.

However, even without the added benefit of indulgences, prayers and actions can be offered for ourselves and for the Souls in Purgatory. Indulgences simply add to those offerings and, in the case of plenary indulgences, may provide an incalculable increase in benefits for the Souls in Purgatory or for ourselves.

CHAPTER 2
A VERY BRIEF HISTORY

I ndulgences are rooted in the Church's authority to bind and loose (Matthew 16:19). The history of Church indulgences goes back hundreds of years. However, many people are aware that, just after the Middle Ages, certain abuses in regard to indulgences became widespread, especially in Europe. Martin Luther, supported by others in the Church, condemned those abuses in 1517.

Partly in response, the Church reconfirmed its power to grant indulgences at the Council of Trent in 1563 and tried to reign in those earlier abuses. In particular, it made clear that no one could sell or purchase them as some had done previously. It clarified that indulgences do not replace personal repentance, nor do they substitute for true contrition and conversion.

However, even though the Church had tried to correct abuses earlier, it was not until Pope St. Pius V's Papal Bull in 1567 that strong enough corrective action was finally taken.

Today, some people — especially many Church clergy and many in the hierarchy — still remember the abuses which led to the condemnations of Martin Luther. Even these many years later, there seems to be a residual feeling among some that, if indulgences are encouraged, abuses may occur again — and perhaps that those encouraging their use might themselves be linked with the abuses of old.

Other concerns are also expressed, even by many in the clergy, religious communities and, again, even some in today's hierarchy. Such concerns generally stem from a lack of understanding about indulgences in general and the changes made since the Second Vatican Council.

Prior to 1968, the benefits of partial indulgences were defined in terms of days or years. For example, saying a particular prayer or performing a particular action might be said to gain a partial indulgence of 300 days. Another prayer or action might gain a five year indulgence. Opportunities for gaining both partial and plenary indulgences were numerous.

Since 1968, all of this has changed. No longer are specific periods of days or years assigned to partial indulgences. Opportunities for gaining plenary indulgences are now fewer and the requirements are more restrictive.

Older Catholics who remember the previous regulations, had often learned about indulgences when they were growing up in parochial schools from the good Sisters who taught them. They learned that indulgences can be gained not only for ourselves, but also for the Souls in Purgatory (also called *the Poor Souls*). As children, many Catholics prayed often for the Souls in Purgatory and gained many indulgences for them.

(The first authentic application of indulgences, by way of suffrage, to the Souls in Purgatory by the Church was documented in 1476 by Pope Sixtus IV.)

However, as many of those children grew into adulthood, their concern and prayers for the Souls in Purgatory faded. They heard little about indulgences at Mass — or at any other time. Some people thought that indulgences might have been discontinued, or perhaps just used by older religious people who still understood them.

Today, indulgences are rarely taught, either in the Catholic school system or to adults. Even if they are brought up, their mention is frequently brief. Most adults have not heard a word about them in years. Some might understandably assume that they no longer exist. After all, if they did still exist — and were actually important — surely priests, religious, or *someone* would be talking about them!

Indulgences do still exist, although their form has undergone significant and meaningful changes. But what has not changed is their tremendous value both for us and to help the Souls in Purgatory.

What follows is a summary of the current status of indulgences since 1968. This now little known and seldom used tool can be very powerful, not only for helping ourselves and the Souls in Purgatory, but actually for changing our everyday lives to become more closely aligned with what God wants of us.

Working to obtain indulgences is a practice in the unselfish giving of ourselves to others in need: the Souls in Purgatory. As the giving of ourselves for the Poor Souls in Purgatory becomes a habit, so will the giving of ourselves to each other in our daily lives on earth.

That is because the habits which are developed in obtaining indulgences create a stronger awareness of God and a healthier spirituality in our daily lives. Such is fully separate from the efficacy of indulgences in making up for punishment due to forgiven sins for both ourselves and for the Poor Souls. Indulgences only add to that.

Our sincere work to regularly gain indulgences can become a very real practice in healthy day-to-day Christian living.

CHAPTER 3
MANY PEOPLE ARE CONFUSED ABOUT INDULGENCES

I t is not the intent of this book to debate the entire theology of indulgences, nor is its intent to explore in detail the past history of this doctrine. Our present purpose is to look at the Church's *current* teachings so that those who may wish to use them will have information on their current regulations.

Interestingly, in recent years, many lay people and clergy have developed an unusual attitude regarding the Church's teaching on indulgences. As mentioned before, not content with simply ignoring this special aid, provided by the Church for us, some people go so far as to voice strong personal convictions in opposition to them. Sadly, as I repeatedly note, that continues to include some Catholic clergy.

Such people may complain that indulgences are not adequately founded in theology and that the Church can not really justify continuing the doctrine. Such people would rather direct people to what *they themselves* have determined to be the only important areas of Church teaching.

What these people don't realize is that such attitudes can cause spiritual damage both to themselves and to others. Such damage is done on three fronts:

First, an important aid to our spiritual strength and growth is ignored. That's because, as we perform an indulgenced action or say an indulgenced prayer, we must do so with an appropriate humble and sincere heart. Going through the motions without the correct frame of heart and mind will not gain for us the benefits of the indulgence.

Second, an important means to remember and assist the Church Suffering, the Souls in Purgatory, is lost. Not only is it a help for the Poor Souls — the Souls in Purgatory — but we ourselves can receive invaluable help to reduce suffering for *our own* forgiven sins.

Third, loyalty and support for both the Church and the Holy Father can be damaged by minimizing and even attacking this established doctrine. After all, even in current times, popes themselves continue to promulgate new indulgences for the faithful.

All of this can weaken the Church as a whole in a time when strength and unity in the Church is especially important.

In almost every case, people who have developed such negative or indifferent attitudes have done so without learning — or even wishing to learn — the foundation and fundamentals of the Church's current teaching on indulgences.

Vatican II did not mention the Church's teaching on indulgences. However, almost immediately after its completion, Pope Paul VI wrote strongly in support of the Church's teachings on indulgences — and approved the newly revised regulations. Those revisions to the regulations on indulgences came out immediately on the heels of the just completed Vatican II — and may well have been positively affected by it.

~

A number of questions and concerns on indulgences will be addressed in Part Two of this book: *Questions and Answers.*

CHAPTER 4

INDULGENCES AND THE 12TH GRADE

Mrs. Lee, a 12th grade teacher, established a grading policy at the beginning of the year for her students. She said that if a student gets at least a B on any test, but wants a higher grade, the student may try to earn one by doing some extra credit work.

The extra credit assignment involves going to the library and picking from one of 70 topics that Mrs. Lee had selected. The student must then write a complete and thoughtful report on the selected topic. It must be a minimum of eight pages in length.

Notice that a student must first get a B on a test in order to even be able to begin an extra credit assignment. Of course, a B isn't a bad grade. In fact, by studying a little harder, a student might be able to get an A instead of a B and not worry about doing an extra credit assignment at all.

Now, take a look at how this analogy might relate to the Church's regulations on indulgences.

Praying or offering something up in penance for our sins or for the Souls in Purgatory is good. Just as a B for the student is good, so are our prayers and offerings.

So the question arises: Is it really necessary to get an A? And is it necessary for one's prayers to be any more meaningful or efficacious [effective] than they already are?

In many cases, a student might be satisfied with the B. But, in other cases, an A might be more important, even *very* important. Perhaps a student's grade point average must be kept high in order to be accepted into a certain program or college after high school.

So the student has two choices: Do more studying before the big test, or earn extra credit later.

We also have two choices: We can pray even more, do more penance, and increase our spirituality to gain what indulgences could otherwise offer. Or, we can work to obtain indulgences to further increase the benefits obtained through our prayer and sacrifices.

People can work and pray harder to try to gain what indulgences offer. But how do you work hard enough *to be sure* you have gained the benefits of, for example, a plenary indulgence, either for yourself or for a soul in Purgatory?

Sinners that we all are, some of us could work our whole lives and never gain everything that one properly obtained plenary indulgence can offer.

Is it necessary for the student to get an A? Usually not. Is it necessary for us to gain plenary indulgences? Possibly not. But both are *desirable*. And if we are the ones suffering in Purgatory, as many of us might be one day, reducing our pain and suffering would be more than an optional luxury for us.

Let's add one more variable here. Let's assume that the teacher is using a blind grading system. (Such systems exist.) In this case, students are told whether they have any problems they need to work on. But the students are not allowed to see their individual grades. They don't know *for sure* how they are doing.

In this situation, some students will wish to do something to help ensure that they receive the highest grade possible — even though they don't know what that might be.

So students might choose to do the extra credit anyway.

Indulgences are the same. We don't always know the degree our prayers and works might be helping the Souls in Purgatory — or ourselves. We, too, might want to do something to try to ensure the maximum benefits from our prayers and works. We can use indulgences to help us.

Indulgences are not a Church requirement. Really, they are not even extra credit. They are a way we can *increase our spirituality* and benefit from the extra merits earned by Jesus and the saints as part of the spiritual treasury dispensed by the Church.

Nonetheless, we can work to obtain indulgences to help us. They can indeed increase the benefits of our prayers and sacrifices in order to help us, or the Souls in Purgatory, in the next life.

Many people find the benefits obtainable through indulgences to be well worth the spiritual effort required.

Look more closely at those 12th grade "extra credits." If a student selected a topic that was not on the list of topics given by the teacher, and then wrote just three pages instead of the required eight pages, would the teacher be likely to give the student extra credit for the assignment? Probably not.

Would we think that the teacher was being unfair?

Of course not. It is her class, and her extra credit. She can set it up anyway that she wants. Other teachers don't even provide their students with such an option.

Church indulgences are the same. The Church can dispense the merits of Christ and of the saints using any standards the Church wishes. To indiscriminately give out these merits without being earned would make it likely that such merits would not be understood or valued, nor would it be likely that an accompanying growth in spirituality would take place at all.

Jesus gave His Church the keys to the kingdom. He let the Church set things up, so long as they do not contradict what He taught. Jesus doesn't micromanage the Church. That's why He turned it over to Peter on which He built His Church. Nonetheless, Jesus remains the head of His Church.

Some people might say that God, in His great mercy, would grant such benefits to us just for the asking. But, while taking into account God's mercy, such people ignore His justice. After all, it is possible that the teacher might give an A to the student anyway, even though the extra credit project wasn't completed properly. But it certainly isn't as likely as it would be if the extra credit had been completed properly.

From a theological perspective, the comparison of indulgences to extra credit in a classroom is not accurate. However, it might help some people picture this a bit more easily.

Why do some people fight the simple procedures the Church has given us to complete an indulgence? Do such people get a regular printout from God showing them what punishment they have left to complete for their sins? Do they get regular updates on how their prayers are helping the Souls in Purgatory — if they remember to pray for them at all? Is there a reason why these people think it is unnecessary or perhaps even beneath them to take part in the spiritual growth possible simply by working to obtain indulgences?

Of course, some students always complain about assignments. Why can't the assignment be three pages instead of eight? Won't they learn the same thing? Why can't they just pick their own topic? Isn't their topic just as educational and important for their grade as what their teacher chooses?

Likely not.

In the same way, some people complain about the Church's regulations on indulgences. Why do we have to do this or that? Does God really care as long as our hearts are in the right place?

Students normally don't get away with such complaining — and we don't either.

Now let's add a last variable. Instead of the teacher giving the extra credit assignment, let's say that the student's *parents* give it. However, even though the parents give the assignment, it's the *teacher* who will still give the grade. Will an arrangement like that work?

Early in the school year, the teacher, Mrs. Lee, met with all the parents to tell them how her grading system worked. She gave the parents the authority to design such appropriate extra credit assignments as they felt would best help their children.

Didn't Jesus give the authority to His Church to do the same thing? Isn't the Church able to choose appropriate prayers and actions, under the guidance of the Holy Spirit, which would best support God's children's spiritual strength and growth?

Or must the Church submit everything to Jesus for approval?

Of course not.

Would students' parents be doing their children a favor by requiring an extra credit assignment that would be so easy as to provide no benefit for students? They would not be. Nor would such parents be acting in the best interest of their children by creating a project so hard that it could not be understood or accomplished by them.

For some reason, some people — even some clergy — are not willing to acknowledge the authority of the Church in this area.

Perhaps if these people would study the current regulations and understand the benefits of using indulgences, rather than engaging in unproductive theoretical discussions based on past history and personal misunderstandings, more Souls in Purgatory would be helped — and more people might reduce the punishment due for their own sins.

Admittedly, this "extra credit" analogy may not be a good one in understanding all aspects of indulgences. But perhaps it might provide a partial perspective into at least some of the misunderstood aspects of indulgences. We will look at additional examples in Chapter 12 and again in Part Two.

The Church's doctrine of indulgences provides a structure that can help many people to increase the quality and quantity of their prayers and charitable works. Done frequently, we can develop and practice a pattern, a habit, of Christian living that can be carried over in our lives even when indulgences are not being obtained.

Constructive discussions of certain doctrines can lead to clarification and a strengthening regarding certain situations in life. However, an overt and unproductive failure to support the Church and the Holy Father in this, or in any doctrine, can lead to a weakening of an individual's faith and the unity of the Body of Christ itself. This is especially true of doctrines which, as here, can lead to a strengthening of our spiritual lives.

The design of indulgences gives us a structure to support our own spiritual well-being — and for helping the souls suffering in Purgatory.

Catholics do not generally question the Sacrament of Penance. It is understood that, with proper contrition, sins are forgiven through the intermediary of the priest. But we don't think that God is being forced to forgive our sins in confession.

Scripture is clear that *"Whose sins you forgive are forgiven them; and whose sins you retain are retained* (John 20:22-23)."

But, if the penitent in confession is not sincere, if intentional lies are told to the priest, if the penitent's contrition is not adequately sincere and the penance given is treated as a sham by the penitent, then sins are not forgiven through this sacrament. True, the priest says the words of absolution but, before God, it is possible that the penitent's sins may not have been forgiven.

In some ways, indulgences are similar. Using the general authority granted to it by Christ, the Church has established indulgences to reduce or eliminate the *punishment* owed due to forgiven sins. Is God being *required* to reduce such punishment? Certainly no more than He is required to forgive the guilt of unrepentant sins through the Sacrament of Penance. God is in charge.

If a person wishing to obtain an indulgence is insincere or tries to shortcut requirements, then, in the eyes of God, it is possible that the punishment might not be reduced or eliminated. God is not compelled to do anything. We can only rely on His mercy and goodness to give to us and to the suffering Souls in Purgatory graces that we still might not truly deserve.

As much as people like to think that they can function freely without restraints or structure, the truth is that people, both as individuals and as a society, function happier and more effectively within a structured system of support.

CHAPTER 5
INDULGENCES IN PERSPECTIVE

I ndulgences should not be thought of as something to "collect." Rather, they are a means of encouraging and enriching a fuller life — with God always at our life's center. By encouraging us to consistently lift our minds and hearts to God, all of our actions are enriched, regardless of the presence or absence of indulgences.

If we then offer those actions to God, either for the remission of the punishment due for our own sins, or for the Souls in Purgatory, those actions become richer and all the more meaningful. The Church recognizes the strength of such actions and prayers by further enriching them from the spiritual treasury of merits and graces won by Christ and the saints — through indulgences.

That enrichment and reception of grace through such God-centered actions and prayers, which already come with their own graces, are what indulgences are really about.

Of course, the Church could have chosen not to indulgence any actions and prayers. And a person whose life is centered around God can and should still choose to offer those same works and prayers to God as penance for sins.

Surely, God would still look with favor upon such offerings which we properly and freely give to God.

In establishing its regulations on indulgences, the Church, in her goodness, concretely recognizes, encourages, and enriches our lives, prayers, and works when undertaken with God at their center.

Indulgences, then, boost the merits and graces we may already obtain as we live and act within the aura of God. They may apply to a single action, to a series of prayers and actions, or to our ongoing daily lives in God.

Indulgences encourage living our lives as Christ taught us — in faith, in hope, and in love.

It is certainly not necessary to be concerned about indulgencing our actions at every moment. However, it *is* important to look for ways to live every moment in God's will and love — and not in our own.

However, becoming excessively preoccupied with obtaining indulgences without an accompanying growth in spirituality can mean neglecting other important parts of our lives. It can take our minds and hearts away from a connection to God — the exact opposite of what indulgences are there to do for us.

Even though they aren't necessary, neglecting indulgences can lose for us a help in remembering our own sinfulness and the need to do penance for our sins. Tragically, it can also mean neglecting the suffering Souls in Purgatory — who have only us to rely upon for help.

∽

The *Manual of Indulgences (4th Edition)* specifically says:

"*The Apostolic Penitentiary therefore, rather than stress the repetition of formulas and acts, has been concerned to put greater emphasis on the Christian way of life and to focus attention on cultivating a spirit of prayer and penance and on the exercise of the theological virtues.*"

That is the crux of the indulgence process. It is what can make all of this so important in our daily lives.

CHAPTER 6
PREREQUISITES

The Church has established several general requirements in order for a person to be capable of obtaining any indulgence. As we will see later, plenary indulgences, as well as specific prayers and actions, may have their own additional requirements.

A person must:

1. Be baptized;

2. Not be excommunicated from the Church;

3. Be in the state of grace, at least at the completion of the prescribed works;

4. Have at least the general intention to obtain the indulgence.

5. Be a subject of the one granting the indulgence.

6. Have the correct disposition when performing the required work or prayer at the prescribed time and manner. This can vary depending on the indulgence. It may be that we must have a contrite heart, raise our mind in humble trust to God, have a spirit of faith or penance, or a similar

sincere disposition towards God — as might be required by
the indulgence.

~

THE INTENTION. Although the *Manual of Indulgences* itself
does not discuss the type of intention required, the Church
generally recognizes that there can be different ways to have
an intention. For example, instead of needing to have a
specific intention to gain an indulgence at the exact time
that someone does the work necessary to gain the indulgence, a person might make a daily intention each morning
to obtain all indulgences possible throughout the day, as
permitted by the Church.

General intentions might technically be good until
revoked (i.e.: by mortal sin or other events). However, the
actual intention and quality of seldom-made intentions may
be forgotten or fade over even a short time.

Therefore, it is most efficacious (best) if the intention is
renewed often. They are best made at the time of the indulgenced prayers or works. Fresh and frequent intentions
might also improve the quality and efficacy of the indulgence itself.

CHAPTER 7
PARTIAL INDULGENCES

P artial indulgences now do one thing only: They boost the remission of punishment normally gained by any indulgenced action or prayer. They add an equal amount of merits and graces as the indulgenced prayer or action earns without the indulgence.

Therefore, the greater degree of charity and good in the action performed, the proportionally greater will be the remission of temporal punishment gained through the partial indulgence from that indulgenced action or prayer.

A partial indulgence, then, doubles whatever indeterminate grace and merits were separately earned from such indulgenced prayer or action.

Even without the indulgence, such actions can still be important means of "purification and sanctification" either for the one performing the action or prayer, or for the Souls in Purgatory if offered for them.

The Church points out that there are things that are *"necessary or at least better and more efficacious for the attainment of salvation."*

Salvation is always more important than release from

any punishment due for our sins. Without first securing salvation, there can be no release from punishment after our death.

As an example of a partial indulgence, if a person were to offer up for himself, or for a soul in Purgatory, the discomfort experienced while outside pulling weeds on a cold and damp day, even without an indulgence attached a certain undefined amount of remission for punishment due for our sins would be gained. That is valuable.

But, if a pious invocation, such as *"All for Thee,"* is added while raising the mind humbly to God, and if one has the intention to gain the indulgence — under the First General Grant (below) — the amount of remission gained from both the action and invocation, together with the indulgence, is doubled.

A partial indulgence, then, doubles any (undefined amount of) remission for punishment due to (forgiven) sins which is otherwise gained by any indulgenced prayer or action.

Specific times in days or years are no longer assigned as had been done years ago. You will still find those times in days or years in older books and writings. But they are not applicable today.

It is simply a "partial indulgence."

The greater degree of charity and good shown by the one performing an indulgenced action, the proportionally greater will be the remission of temporal punishment through any partial indulgence gained for that action.

Nonetheless, as already said, even without the indulgence, such actions and prayers can still be important means of "purification and sanctification" for the one performing the action or for the Souls in Purgatory.

However, gaining our own salvation is of prime importance. We should also be praying for the salvation of other sinners in the world, even though indulgences themselves are not applicable for those intentions.

THE GENERAL CONCESSIONS
(Previously, the General Grants)

There are four general concessions (formerly, but still also called: general grants) of partial indulgences which deal primarily with the everyday living of a Christian life. An additional category involves specific prayers and actions.

Done regularly with sincerity and from the heart, these General Grants of Indulgences can make one's life a prayer.

They allow us to *"pray without ceasing"* (1 Thessalonians 5:17).

THE FIRST GENERAL GRANT (or Concession)
(Daily Life Indulgences)[1]

A partial indulgence is granted to the Christian faithful who, while carrying out their duties and enduring the hardships of life, raise their minds in humble trust to God and make, at least mentally, some pious invocation.

---

1. As are the other grants, this is the author's designation for the First General Grant. It is not found in the *Manual of Indulgences*.

–from the *Manual of Indulgences* (4th ed)

This is an exciting category of partial indulgences since it encourages an ongoing daily lifting of our minds to God in humble trust in everything that we do. It does not require, as some people used to complain, a ritualized or routine format to gain the indulgence.

The pious invocations themselves are not individually indulgenced. Rather, it is the package which makes up a healthy spiritual life that leads us to a continuing pattern of living within the framework which Christ Himself established for us. It encourages an ongoing, daily love for God and for others in all that we do.

Daily Life Indulgences permit us to offer up our every daily work, action, struggle, and suffering to obtain a partial indulgence for ourselves or for the Souls in Purgatory, depending on for which intention we offer it.

Together with the Third General Grant, this is an example of the tradition of *"offering it up"* for the Souls in Purgatory, or as penance for our own sins.

Even by itself, this one general grant (concession) can make life itself a prayer. In combination with the other indulgences allowed by the Church, and a true dedication to God, one's life truly can become a prayer.

In order to gain this partial indulgence, four things are necessary:

1. Performance of a duty of life or bearing one of life's burdens. Naturally, these actions should be consistent with Christian values.

2. Raising the mind in humble trust to God.

3. The addition, with a contrite heart, of some pious invocation. This may be added aloud or just mentally. (See Appendix A for examples of such invocations.)

4. The intention to obtain the indulgence.

THE SECOND GENERAL GRANT
(Works of Charity/Good Works Indulgences)[2]

A partial indulgence is granted to the faithful who, led by the spirit of faith, give compassionately of themselves or of their goods to serve their brothers in need.

–from the *Manual of Indulgences* (4th ed)

This category permits partial indulgences to be gained by performing works of charity. All such works might be indulgenced when obtained as Daily Life Indulgences, but here a special category is established for particular kinds of good works.

This indulgence involves a personal giving of oneself or of one's goods to help other people who are in need.

Indeed, the *Manual of Indulgences* is clear that *"not all works of charity are enriched with this indulgence, but only works that 'serve their brothers in need'..."* (Emphasis added.)

As examples, this might include driving someone to the store, church, or some other place they need to go when

---

2. This is the author's designation for the Second General Grant.

having no transportation of their own available. It can mean giving some of your own food to someone who needs it. It might mean providing comfort and assurance to someone who is struggling emotionally or spiritually in life. It might involve taking the time to teach something to someone who needs to learn and needs you to help them.

There are clearly many such opportunities to gain these indulgences. And it is exciting that the Church has chosen to indulgence actions for which Christ Himself provided the example and which lead us to an ongoing awareness of opportunities to become more Christlike. We are again provided the opportunity and encouragement to live each day — and offer all that we do — as a prayer.

To obtain this partial indulgence, two things are required:
   1. Performance of a good work for someone in need;
   2. The intention to obtain the indulgence.

THE THIRD GENERAL GRANT
(Abstention Indulgences)[3]

A partial indulgence is granted to the Christian faithful who, in a spirit of penance, voluntarily abstain from something that is licit for and pleasing to them.

–from the *Manual of Indulgences* (4th ed)

---

3.   This is the author's designation for the Third General Grant.

Abstention Indulgences allow us the opportunity to follow Christ by giving up those things which are pleasing to us for the reparation of punishment due to sins. Here is an opportunity to strengthen our self-control over the desires and weaknesses of our bodies and desires. The fact that a means to strengthen our virtue through self-denial is also indulgenced, may make it foolish for us not to make full use of this category of indulgences.

This grant indulgences "giving things up" for the Souls in Purgatory, or for the punishment still due for our own sins. The Church is encouraging opportunities for unselfish giving, self-denial, and for returning to the example of Christ.

To obtain this indulgence, the thing to be given up must be something that is believed to be permitted and available to have. It must also be desired and pleasing to the person.

Obviously, there would likely not be an indulgence for giving up an item of food that one doesn't like anyway. However, eating that food might still gain a Daily Life Indulgence (the First General Grant) if the proper spirit and intention are present — combined with a pious invocation.

The powerful combination of prayerful fasts throughout the year, now so often neglected, is made even more meaningful for the Poor Souls by seeking an indulgence in conjunction with our fast. Of course, fasts are not restricted to giving up food alone. For many, giving up one's near addiction to social media, television, or other pleasures may also be worthy fasts to undertake.

Spontaneously giving up a dessert one has been looking forward to, giving up the comfort of an air conditioner or heater (while not damaging health) even for just a few minutes, not eating candy or buying a soda when you would have done so without otherwise thinking about it...

There are many such opportunities during the day to turn our thoughts away from the distractions of life and unselfishly offer even these little things up for those souls who have only us to pray for them.

Christ had many occasions when He could have made life easier for Himself. The Evil One knew that when he tempted Jesus in the desert. But Jesus provided the example for us that it is important to take the more difficult path of self-denial for the greater good of our souls — and as an example to others.

In order to obtain this partial indulgence, three things are required:

1. Abstaining from something that is pleasing to us and permitted for us to have;

2. A spirit of penance;

3. The intention to obtain the indulgence.

THE FOURTH GENERAL GRANT
(Witness of Faith Indulgence)[4]

A partial indulgence is granted to the Christian faithful who, in the particular circumstances of daily life, voluntarily give explicit witness to their faith before others.

–from the *Manual of Indulgences* (4th ed)

---

4. This is the author's designation for the Fourth General Grant.

At least in America, Catholics are not widely known as a Church that witnesses about its faith openly to others. Various other Christian churches are more commonly known for their ongoing witnesses, whether knocking on doors, or confidently testifying to their belief in Jesus to others. A number of them can find themselves talking to people who don't welcome them at all.

Most people don't know it today but, many years ago in some places in America, Catholic men used to go door-to-door on weekends quietly inviting people to talk with them and to find out about the Catholic Church.

Do you know of any Catholics doing that in America today? In many cases, such people would find fallen away Catholics whom they would encourage to return to the Church. There are many fallen away Catholics. Rarely, do we see that sort of outreach today. Indeed, I have seen some Catholics actively discourage it.

Catholics tend to be quiet — sometimes, too quiet — about their faith.

This grant is flexible in that it does not describe to whom or in what situations a witness of faith must be given — other than *voluntarily "in the particular circumstances of daily life."* (This indulgence does not require us to go door-to-door sharing our faith — although that can certainly be indulgenced.)

This indulgence encourages us to be an active witness to others, explicitly testifying about our personal belief in Jesus Christ as our Savior.

In order to gain a partial indulgence under the Fourth General Grant, two things are required:

1. In daily life, voluntarily give explicit witness to one's faith before other people;

2. Have the intention to gain the indulgence.

∼

As was said when we started this chapter, when done regularly — and sincerely from the heart — the previous four General Grants of Indulgences can effectively make our lives a prayer. That, alone, is what can make the entire process of indulgences so valuable.

CHAPTER 8
INDULGENCED PRAYERS AND ACTIONS

E ven though the prayers and works of partial indulgences are no longer assigned specified days or years, a number of specific prayers and actions are nonetheless enriched with either partial or plenary indulgences.

The authentic collection of prayers and pious works to which indulgences are attached is found in the current *Manual of Indulgences*. A sampling of them is found in the appendices to this book.

Partial Indulgences

To obtain these partial indulgences, two things are required:

1. Saying the indulgenced prayer or performing the indulgenced action as described in the *Manual of Indulgences*.

2. The intention to obtain the indulgence.

CHAPTER 9
A SUMMARY OF PARTIAL INDULGENCES

Partial indulgences free us or a soul in Purgatory from part of the punishment due to sins already forgiven. *They cannot be gained for another living person,* only for ourselves or the Souls in Purgatory.

Adding equal merits and graces to what we might earn through specific indulgenced prayers, works, and grants, partial indulgences effectively double what would be the normal, *indeterminate reduction* of punishment due to sins otherwise gained from the various grants, prayers, and actions as described by the Church.

A. In order to gain a partial indulgence within the First General Grant, four things are necessary:

1. Performance of a duty of life or bearing one of life's burdens;

2. Raising the mind in humble trust to God;

3. The addition, with a contrite heart, of some pious invocation aloud or just mentally;

4. The intention to obtain the indulgence.

B. In order to gain a partial indulgence within the Second General Grant, two things are required:
   1. Performance of a good work for someone in need;
   2. The intention to obtain the indulgence.

C. In order to gain a partial indulgence within the Third General Grant, three things are required:
   1. Abstaining from something that is pleasing to us and is permitted for us to have;
   2. A spirit of penance;
   3. The intention to obtain the indulgence.

D. In order to gain a partial indulgence within the Fourth General Grant, two things are required:
   1. In daily life, voluntarily give explicit witness to one's faith before other people;
   2. The intention to gain the indulgence.

E. Other Concessions: The requirements to gain partial as well as plenary indulgences for designated, indulgenced prayers and actions are specifically described in the *Manual of Indulgences*. (Additional, often one-time indulgences are periodically granted by the Apostolic See.)
   In order to gain these indulgences, one must:
   1. Choose and perform a specific indulgenced action or say a specified indulgenced prayer as described in the *Manual of Indulgences;*

2. Have the intention to gain the indulgence.

3. In the case of plenary indulgences, complete the additional requirements for such indulgences.

CHAPTER 10
PLENARY INDULGENCES

Why all these prayers for the departed? Surely, if the soul is in Heaven, there is only cause for celebration! Masses and prayers are not likely to help such a soul since they are obviously in no need of help!

That is a sorrowful assumption were you the one suffering in Purgatory and in need of prayers. So let us now consider the place of plenary indulgences in helping us and the Souls in Purgatory.

Plenary indulgences free a person from ALL of the punishment still due for their sins — *sins which have already been forgiven* (most commonly through confession). Properly gaining a plenary indulgence for a soul in Purgatory might (with provisos) fully end their time there. In other cases, it might simply allow them to enter Heaven more quickly, although the soul may still remain in Purgatory a while longer — for example, for sins which were not previously forgiven.

Note that plenary indulgences can also release us from the temporal punishment due to our own forgiven sins. Therefore, a periodic effort to secure a plenary indulgence for ourselves seems wise. However, even knowing that, few actually make the serious effort needed to properly obtain one.

It is unfortunate that so many people do not understand the meaning and strength of a plenary indulgence. Upon the death of a loved one, many people are sure to say a Rosary and have one or more Masses offered for the departed soul.

Loving relatives and close friends long to know whether their loved one is yet in Heaven. Some ask a priest for help and consolation. Most frequently, people assume that their loved ones are in Heaven. After all, wasn't he (or she) a good person?

That assumption can be a sad one since, should they be in Purgatory, they will likely get no prayers at all. Nor do most priests and clergy even think of suggesting getting indulgences for them. Too often, the opportunity to gain a plenary indulgence for a soul is never even considered. If it were, it would almost assuredly require teaching about indulgences... that is, if the priest himself is knowledgeable and supportive of them. Indulgences fell out of favor with too many of the clergy, including many priests and bishops, many, many years ago.

I should add that priests and other clergy might also find themselves in Purgatory. It is important not to forget offering prayers and obtaining indulgences for them, not just once, but in an ongoing effort to be sure that God might bring them to Heaven more quickly.

Although many of the faithful think they are, our clergy are not automatically saints just because they have taken solemn vows of Holy Orders. They are people like us. We need to remember them, too. We are all just imperfect people struggling together to do God's will and to get to

Heaven. They chose to serve us. We should also serve them, especially after their death.

Do we know whether someone is in Purgatory — or somewhere else? Generally, we do not.

We should truly hope that our loved ones — and others we don't know, but for whom we should also pray — are either in Heaven or Purgatory. The remaining option is not a good one.

Therefore, we should err on the side of continued prayers and indulgences for loved ones who pass away rather than just assuming that they were so good, and that God is so forgiving, that they are already in Heaven.

Were you in Purgatory, you would appreciate prayers at your death and at your funeral, but you would be begging for prayers well beyond that. Some may continue grieving for you — but without prayers to God asking that you be brought to Heaven more quickly.

Since we cannot always know when we can safely stop praying for a soul in Purgatory, we should not just regularly remember specific souls — but also the Poor Souls generally in our prayers and in the prayerful activities of our daily lives. We can easily do so through the General Grants for partial indulgences.

If an unfortunate soul should be condemned to Hell, no amount of prayers can help — although some of us ask God for His mercy anyway.

Clearly, the only souls who can be helped by the prayers of the faithful are those souls suffering in Purgatory — and only rarely can we be fully certain where these souls are.

The Church tells us that a plenary indulgence will free a soul from the remaining punishment due to forgiven sins and may allow the soul to enter Heaven.

Even if a plenary indulgence is undertaken, but not

completed successfully, those prayers can still be of great help to a soul in Purgatory. Normally, an incomplete plenary indulgence will default to a partial indulgence. Either way, suffering souls can be helped.

Is it that people do not want to believe the Church when it tells them that such indulgences really exist? They are part of the Church's spiritual treasury of grace and merits earned by Jesus and the saints who had offered their suffering to God and obtained grace beyond what were needed — as they gave their lives and their love to and for God.

Are people unaware of the existence or value of these indulgences today?

Yes, they are.

Could it be that bishops, priests, and religious are themselves so unaware or unconvinced of the value of a plenary indulgence that they no longer discuss or encourage its use among the faithful?

That is too often true. That has contributed to the decline of awareness and use of all indulgences, but especially the plenary indulgence.

However, note that even if indulgences "aren't real," as some people continue to think, the very act and process of working to get them creates, by design, stronger spirituality in us all.

Of course, none of this in any way diminishes the power and magnitude of the Mass and other prayers. Indeed, most people are still unaware of just how much can be accomplished through unceasing prayer combined with a strong faith and love for God. Our Lady has said that the best prayer is the Mass itself.

The excellence and importance of the Mass and prayers for the dead cannot be overstated. The Church recognizes the Mass to be foremost among other means of sanctification and purification. Although Masses themselves are not indulgenced, their efficacy for the Souls in Purgatory is invaluable.

Additionally, we must recognize the great value of frequent confession. Confession is critical in the process of obtaining plenary indulgences.

The *Manual of Indulgences* says:

> *"Holy Mother Church, extremely solicitous for the faithful departed, has decided that suffrages can be applied to them to the widest possible extent at any Sacrifice of the Mass..."*

For some people — although fewer today — Masses and prayers for a single soul can seemingly become their life's work when, often unknown to them, a properly obtained plenary indulgence can significantly add to that work by drawing on the vast treasures of grace that Christ and the saints have gained for us — and help to more quickly bring an end to that soul's time in Purgatory.

As another indicator of the overall importance of the indulgence process in our spiritual lives, we read this from Pope Paul VI:

> *"The faithful who apply indulgences as suffrages for the dead are practicing charity in a superior way and with their thoughts on the things of heaven are dealing more virtuously with the things of earth."[1]*

---

1. As found in the commentary following Canon 994, sourced from the *Enchiridion indulgentiarum #3: Documents on the Liturgy* (1963-1979) #3195.

Although the Mass itself is not indulgenced, indulgences may be connected to the Mass when participating on specific occasions, such as a First Communion, the First Mass of a newly ordained priest — or in some other specially defined and connected way.

Since 1968, the opportunities to gain plenary indulgences have been reduced and the general requirements have been strengthened. This has now made the gaining of each plenary indulgence even more meaningful. But each such indulgence can still help to release a soul from Purgatory, or satisfy the temporal punishment due for our own forgiven sins.

People should take the time necessary to properly prepare themselves so that they can actually obtain a plenary indulgence. In the past, people did not always pay attention to being properly disposed. As a result, they may not have actually obtained the indulgence. The structure of the new norms supports a more complete preparation.

GAINING PLENARY INDULGENCES

Although at least 44+ specific prayers and works leading to plenary indulgences are listed in the *Manual of Indulgences* (4th edition), only *one* plenary indulgence may be obtained per day. The one exception is that a plenary indulgence may be obtained at the moment of death, even if another plenary indulgence had been obtained on the same day.

Prayers and good works which may be used to gain a plenary indulgence include such things as: adoration of the Blessed Sacrament for at least half an hour; saying the Rosary in certain situations, partly including in a church or in a family; making the Way of the Cross; reading or listening to Sacred Scripture for at least half an hour; and many more. Some samples are included in the Appendix to this book.

A reminder that all details and the authentic list of prayers and pious works to which plenary indulgences are attached are found in the *Manual of Indulgences.*

~

In order to gain a plenary indulgence, it is necessary to fulfill five conditions:

1. A prescribed prayer or work to which a plenary indulgence is attached must be completed. There are many which can be chosen.

2. The Sacrament of Penance (Reconciliation; Confession) must be received. All of the other conditions must be performed for *each* plenary indulgence. However, only one confession is needed in order to gain more than one plenary indulgence.

Specifically, the *Manual of Indulgences* says, "*A single sacramental confession suffices for gaining several plenary indulgences...*"

Confession should, therefore, be up to *several* days before or after the completion of the prescribed work.

It is clear that people who wish to obtain a plenary indulgence on a *daily* basis must go to confession often.

~

I pause here to look at the word, "several." That word is the only description in the *Manual of Indulgences* to give us a clue as to how many days is acceptable or permissible prior to the indulgenced work.

So, just how many days away from the indulgenced work are we talking about? Over the years, we have seen different estimates. Although, in the past — and as just examples — we have heard both two weeks and eight days. However, at this time, "several" may now be defined as up to 20 days.[2]

On January 29, 2000, the Apostolic Penitentiary released, *The Gift Of The Indulgence.* In part, it says:

> "It is appropriate, but not necessary, that the sacramental Confession and especially Holy Communion and the prayer for the Pope's intentions take place on the same day that the indulgenced work is performed; but it is sufficient that these sacred rites and prayers be carried out within several days (about 20) before or after the indulgenced act...."[3]

I personally believe that it is not just appropriate but is, whenever possible, *ideal* if confession — along with communion and prayers for the Pope's intentions — take place on the same day, or as close as possible, to the indulgenced work. I would encourage that whenever it is possible. (How-

2. Note that most people would likely not consider "20" days to be "several" — the term used in the current *Manual of Indulgences*. Uncertainty regarding how far confession can be from the indulgenced action has been with us for many years.
3. If still available, see the following. Note that the 20 day reference is in the *General Remarks On Indulgences* section, not in the subsequent the *Specific Aspects of the Jubilee Year* section.

https://www.vatican.va/roman_curia/tribunals/apost_penit/documents/rc_trib_appen_pro_20000129_indulgence_en.html ever, if serious sin is present, confession must be prior to the indulgenced work.)

∾

3. Reception of Holy Communion.

4. Prayers for the intentions of the Pope: The faithful are free to recite any prayers "*according to individual piety and devotion*" (*Manual of Indulgences*). Reciting one Our Father and one Hail Mary for the Pope's intentions would fulfill this condition, although other prayers may also be selected. This condition may be *in addition* to any prayers prescribed as part of the work itself.

For example, the *Manual of Indulgences* states that when a prescribed work for acquiring a plenary indulgence involves a devout visit to a church or oratory, the person obtaining the indulgence must recite one Our Father and the Creed. But the *Manual of Indulgences* is not clear as to whether or not the recitation of these prayers also satisfies the requirement of prayers for the intentions of the Pope.

Although it is considered best that communion be received and the prayers for the Pope's intentions be said on the same day that the prescribed work is performed, these conditions, too, may be fulfilled several days before or after the performance of the work. But remember that, although a single confession is all that is needed to obtain several plenary indulgences, communion and prayers for the Pope's intentions must be done for *each* plenary indulgence.

. . .

5. The final requirement to obtain a plenary indulgence is perhaps the most difficult for many people. It is regularly overlooked. It is required that *all attachment to sin, even to venial sin, be absent.*

If this disposition is in any way less than complete, or if any of the other conditions are not fulfilled, the indulgence will only be a partial one.

The seemingly imprecise and nebulous wording of this requirement does not appear to require a person to be free of all actual venial sins at the time of the indulgence. Of course, being in the state of grace and free from all *serious* sin is a prerequisite in order to gain any indulgence.

Rather, this requirement tells us that we are not even to be *attached* to sin, even to venial sins. Let's look at an example:

Although the misuse of alcohol can be such that it becomes a serious sin, other times, some condition may be missing so that its abuse might remain a venial sin.

A person might consistently, though perhaps infrequently, abuse alcohol at the lesser degree of seriousness of a venial sin. If that person did not truly wish or intend to permanently stop the behavior which can lead to sin, the *attachment* to that venial sin would prevent the person from obtaining a plenary indulgence. This would be true even if that person were sorry for and had previously confessed all such sins.

One indication of such *attachment* could be that alcohol is still kept available at home, when it could otherwise be disposed of. That is true even if no sin regarding the alcohol is present at the time of the indulgence at all.

The same holds true of someone who unnecessarily keeps other things that encourage or assist sin, such as pornographic materials, drug paraphernalia, and so forth —

again, even if sin itself is not present at the time of the indulgence. The mere *attachment* to sin, even without the presence of sin itself, is prohibited by the *Manual of Indulgences* if one is to obtain a plenary indulgence.

So, *no attachment* to sin must be present. This is not to say that a person cannot fall into a particular sin again. Temptations in our struggles in life will always be present. But, at least in regard to plenary indulgences, our sincere desire and intention to sin no more must be complete. And not only this awareness, but the help and love of God may be needed for some of us if such sincere dispositions are to be obtained.

By its nature, this requirement calls for a continuing examination of conscience and of the way one's life flows in working to follow the example of Christ and in keeping the laws of God. It forces us to be aware of all of our shortcomings so that we might work to overcome them through faith, prayer, and an ongoing self-examination.

If there are any sins we do not intend to give up to which we are still attached — even if we are not in sin at the time — we will not be able to successfully obtain a plenary indulgence, although partial indulgences can still be obtained. A good and honest examination of conscience should resolve most concerns people might have about fulfilling this requirement.

People often give short shrift to this last requirement. They don't understand how difficult it can be for many people. Even the clergy haven't always understood not just that one requirement, but the whole process necessary to obtain a plenary indulgence. But the rewards of obtaining one are certainly of enough value that we do our best to get this right.

Nonetheless, we are all imperfect. We can only do the best that we can.

In addition to the above required conditions, the usual prerequisites apply in order to obtain a plenary indulgence, including having the intention to obtain the indulgence.

～

By now, you should understand how much spiritual growth and self-discipline is involved in obtaining indulgences, especially plenary indulgences. That is part of their great value. Yet, today, that is little understood.

So, it is not the indulgence alone which is of great value, although it certainly has great value. It is the work that we do towards a correct disposition as well as the actions needed to gain one.

When practiced on an ongoing basis, that cannot help but to strengthen our personal spirituality and lead to an increase of grace within us. This is an often overlooked reason why indulgences are so important. They can develop the *habit* of spirituality.

But they are seldom understood, encouraged, or used at all today.

Hopefully, that can change.

CHAPTER 11
DIVINE MERCY SUNDAY

N ow we look at the plenary indulgence and, separately, at the promises Jesus has attached to *Divine Mercy Sunday,* which is celebrated on the first Sunday after Easter.

A separate Decree in the *Manual of Indulgences* devotes several pages to a discussion of the *Divine Mercy.* The *Divine Mercy* devotions and, especially, the *Divine Mercy Sunday* promises from Jesus (as well as the separate plenary indulgence) are strongly recommended by the author.[1]

Pope Saint John Paul II granted the following plenary indulgence for *Divine Mercy Sunday:*

"A plenary indulgence, granted under the usual conditions (sacramental confession, Eucharistic communion and prayer for the intentions of [the] Supreme Pontiff) to the faithful who, on the Second Sunday of Easter or Divine Mercy Sunday, in any church or chapel, in a spirit that is completely detached from the

---

1. See the *Divine Mercy* website for more information: https://www.thedivinemercy.org

affection for a sin, even a venial sin, take part in the prayers and
devotions held in honor of Divine Mercy, or who, in the presence
of the Blessed Sacrament exposed or reserved in the tabernacle,
recite the Our Father and the Creed, adding a devout prayer to
the merciful Lord Jesus (e.g. Merciful Jesus, I trust in You!)..."

However, giving *Divine Mercy Sunday* its particular power and importance, we read the following in Saint Faustina Kowalska's *Diary* (#699). Saint Faustina tells us that, in regards to *Divine Mercy Sunday*, Jesus Himself promised:

"The soul that will go to confession and receive Holy Commu-
nion shall obtain complete forgiveness of sins and punishment.
On that day, all the Divine floodgates through which graces
flow are opened. Let no soul fear to draw near to Me, even
though his sins be as scarlet.... Mankind will not have peace
until it turns to the fount of My Mercy."

The plenary indulgence available for this day is a standard plenary indulgence, no different from the others which we have already seen.

What makes this day special are the *promises of Jesus*. Those promises, which are separate from the plenary indulgence, are especially powerful. They should not be ignored.

As would be expected, the plenary indulgence described by Saint John Paul II mentions the usual detachment from all sin, even venial sin. However, the *Diary* of Saint Faustina does not mention that a full detachment from all sin is required for *Divine Mercy Sunday* at all — nor does it mention prayers for the Pope. All that is part of what makes this day so powerful and important for us.[2]

We should not neglect to take advantage of the promises of Jesus for this day. Priests should make every effort to schedule confession as close before, or even on, *Divine Mercy Sunday* as possible. It is best to go to confession just in advance of the day or of the Mass.

On the *www.thedivinemercy.org* website, especially promoted by the *Congregation of Marian Fathers of the Immaculate Conception of the Most Blessed Virgin Mary*, we find the following guidance.

∾

To fittingly observe the Feast of Mercy, we should:

1. *Celebrate the Feast on the Sunday after Easter.*
2. *Sincerely repent of all our sins.*
3. *Place our complete trust in Jesus.*
4. *Go to Confession, preferably before that Sunday.*
5. *Receive Holy Communion on the day of the Feast.*
6. *Venerate the Image of The Divine Mercy.*
7. *Be merciful to others, through our actions, words, and prayers on their behalf.*

∾

The Mass itself is celebrated on *Divine Mercy Sunday* at which, of course, Holy Communion is to be received. (Tech-

---

2. Among other videos and websites, consider watching this video by Father Alar (if still available) about receiving the special graces on Divine Mercy Sunday.

https://www.youtube.com/watch?app=desktop&v=4R2tOEFddig

nically, Jesus's promise doesn't require the Mass, just Holy Communion. However, Mass is required on Sunday anyway. It's part of celebrating the Feast on Sunday.)

Note that the graces — *as well as the requirements* — of the Church's plenary indulgence are *separate* from the graces and promises given by Jesus to Saint Faustina in her private revelations. Unless stated otherwise, don't mix the two. It's easy to do. Even some clergy mix the requirements of a plenary indulgence with the (separate) promise of Jesus to St. Faustina.

Note that while the Divine Mercy given to us from Jesus through His promises, as given to St. Faustina, is directed to us, the plenary indulgence from the Church (with its additional requirements) may be offered either for us or for the Souls in Purgatory.

Indulgences are offered by *the Church, not by Jesus* — other than through the Church's power to bind and loose given to the Church by Jesus.

However, Jesus's Divine Mercy, which is so much in evidence on *Divine Mercy Sunday,* is far more powerful than any indulgence. And it is His Mercy that Jesus offers to us in abundance on *Divine Mercy Sunday* — should we choose to accept it.

CHAPTER 12
A SUMMARY OF PLENARY INDULGENCES

In addition to the usual prerequisites for indulgences, there are six conditions necessary to obtain a plenary indulgence:

1. Proper performance of the prescribed work or prayer;

2. Sacramental confession;

3. Eucharistic communion;

4. Prayers for the intentions of the Pope;

5. The absence of all attachment to sin, even venial sin; and

6. And here's another one: *"A generous disposition of heart."*

――――――――

When reference is made to fulfilling the three "usual" conditions, those three — already included above — are:

1) "Sacramental confession;"

2) "Eucharistic communion;"

3) "Prayer for the intention of the Sovereign Pontiff."

CHAPTER 13
THE PARABLE OF THE SORRY BOY

Here is a another story to help illustrate the meaning and use of indulgences. (This parable is not from Scripture.) Although this analogy is not theologically accurate, it might nonetheless help some to understand the workings of indulgences somewhat better.

~

Eleven year old boys are not perfect.

Although he had been told more than once to stay away from his family's new car while riding his bicycle — and even though it was easy for him to avoid it — John did not. While riding around the new car as fast as he could, he fell into it with his bicycle leaving a long scrape in the beautiful paint on the new car. [Sin never hurts us alone; it often hurts others. But it always hurts God.] To make matters worse, John tore his new pants, scraped his knee, and slightly damaged his bicycle.

Scared, but not knowing what else to do, he went and told his parents what he had done [confession]. Although angry and hurt, they nonetheless realized that their son is more important than the car. His father spoke firmly to John about his failure to follow the rules they had given to him. He told John of their hurt and disappointment.

His father cautioned him not to disobey them again [sin no more] and, of course, John said that he would not. And John meant it! — even though, in the future, he would again break the rules.

John's father forgave his son, but John's father also told John that he would have to make up for his wrong by not being permitted to watch any videos or ride his bicycle for the next ten days. Perhaps others would have given him even greater consequences for it, but John had kind and loving parents. His father also knew that it was out of fairness and love that John must be provided with a structure for his future as he grows up, and for his maturity and self-discipline [as God and the Church do for us]. That's why he insisted on appropriate, but fair consequences.

John may have preferred a spanking, even combined with some other punishment, since he would now miss one of his favorite activities, riding his bicycle — which he did almost every day. He knew that he deserved the punishment because he had been wrong... and he felt bad because he had disappointed and hurt his parents [contrition].

Still, the punishment was a difficult one for John [though nothing compared with that for our own sins and their just punishment in Purgatory].

His father told John that John's mother would oversee John's punishment and could modify it if she felt that it was appropriate. His mother was now given that authority from his father. [The Church, too, has been given authority.]

First thing the next day, John went to his mother [the Church] and suggested that perhaps he could be allowed to ride his bike twice a week — and watch videos once a week — if he cleaned not just his room, but his younger brother's room really well, too. His mother said she knew that his father would agree to that because he is a kind and forgiving man. She felt the arrangement was fair [a Daily Life partial indulgence].

Note that had John just cleaned the rooms without making that arrangement in advance, it would not be as likely that he could have applied it to his punishment. [Instead, he had the advance *intention* to gain the indulgence.] After all, he was supposed to keep his room clean anyway!

However, because he had the intention to gain the indulgence beforehand, by asking to clean his room, and his mother accepted the task in lieu of a portion of the punishment due, John was able to reduce the punishment he had been given, and which he deserved. [This is why we must have the intention to gain each indulgence we would like to obtain *at the time of or prior to* the required prayer or action.]

In love and appreciation, John spontaneously tells his parents in the middle of cleaning his room that he was going to do an especially good job so that they would be proud of him because he knew he had made a mistake. He says that he will do the same for his little brother's room. He then adds some other words, spontaneously, but with sincere feeling, as he tells his mother that he loves her [pious invocation].

Note that if John's attitude had been poor while he was cleaning his room, his mother would not have accepted it in place of his punishment [humility; humble trust]. In the same way, our attitudes must also be sincere in gaining indulgences. Note, too, that if he were just routinely cleaning his room, it is not likely that John would have been as concerned with the quality of his cleaning and the pride of his parents. This is one reason that indulgences are special. They keep our minds on God, who should be the reason for our actions in life.

Later that day, an elderly neighbor comes to visit. She asks John's mother for some help in going to the store so that she can buy some needed food. She can't easily pick up or carry things. John's mother is unable to go at the moment. She mentions her neighbor's need to John who is outside playing with some friends.

John's mother could have simply told John to go to the store but, in her wisdom, she simply makes him aware of the opportunity. Someone is in need.

John independently thinks about it [free will]. He's having a good time with his friends. Nonetheless, he decides that he is willing to give that time up for his mother and for the neighbor who needs help [a Good Works partial indulgence].

Then he does something special. He asks his mother that if he gives up his playing and helps their good, but elderly neighbor, if he can make up for some of the punishment that *his little brother* had earned by talking back to his mother earlier that day. His mother is touched by his offer. She readily agrees, but only to reduce a *part* of his little brother's punishment [as we offer partial indulgences for Souls in Purgatory].

The next day, John realizes that he is going to miss some important videos and not be able to ride his bicycle to meet his friends to play baseball. Again he goes to his mother.

This time, he offers to work in the yard. He says that he will rake up all the leaves, water the lawn, the flowers, and all the plants. He will also do the dreaded job of pulling all the weeds in the garden and flower bed. In addition, he volunteers to help his father to clean the garage.

His mother agrees that he is offering to do a lot of work. She notes that he is sincere and that his attitude is a good one. She says that if he successfully does all that he says he will do, she knows that his father will release him from all of the punishment that he has left. He will again be able to watch videos and ride his bicycle [a plenary indulgence].

However, in order for that to happen, his mother says that he must also fulfill certain conditions.

First, he must maintain his good attitude as he does his work. He must not grumble or complain about the work or say that it is harder than he thought.

Second, he must go to his father and again apologize for his initial disobedience *and for anything else* that John thinks he should tell his father [confession]. She adds that John must also not intend to continue doing things that he knows he is not supposed to do — even little things [no attachment to sin, even to venial sin].

John's mother says that, if she observes that any of these conditions are missing, she will only release him from two additional days of punishment [reduction to a partial indulgence] instead of the remainder of the ten days.

It's a lot, but John willingly agrees to the conditions. He thanks his mother for giving him the opportunity to make up for his punishment [as we should thank Jesus and the Church].

Note something else. This whole episode has been a growing experience for John. He has learned better about right from wrong. He has learned to sacrifice. He has demonstrated love by helping both the neighbor and his brother. He has been made a better person as he grows.

~

It would be nice to say that the young boy whistled his way into the sunset, never again failing to do what he was told to do — never again committing sin.

Alas, he did not.

Nor do we.

.

.

QUESTIONS AND ANSWERS FOLLOW IN PART TWO.

SEE THE APPENDICES FOR SAMPLE INDULGENCES.

∼

Appendix A

Examples of Pious Invocations;
Examples of Partial Indulgences;
Examples of Plenary Indulgences.

Appendix B

Calendar of Indulgences:
List of Specific Days;
Other Special Days;
Other Events.

PART TWO

QUESTIONS AND ANSWERS

PART TWO: TABLE OF CONTENTS

QUESTIONS 1 AND 2

Q1. WON'T PEOPLE JUST TREAT
INDULGENCES LIKE A GAME?
Q2. CAN'T SOME PARTS OF THE
INDULGENCE PROCESS BECOME A
MEANINGLESS ACTIVITY?

Q*UESTION 1.*
Q. AS A PRIEST, I AM CONCERNED THAT
PEOPLE WILL EITHER TREAT GETTING
INDULGENCES AS A GAME, SEEING HOW MANY
THEY CAN ACCUMULATE, OR PERHAPS THAT INDUL-
GENCES WILL JUST BECOME ROUTINE AND MEAN-
INGLESS.

A. At least in part, it may be this concern which has caused
some Catholic clergy, even some bishops, to avoid the teaching, and even personal use of indulgences. Certainly this
may stem from a lack of understanding concerning the
current regulations and the importance of indulgences for
the faithful — as an aid for ourselves, and for the Souls in
Purgatory.

Of course, there may be people who might appear to
misuse or abuse the privilege of indulgences just as there
will always be some people who, even though their inten-

tions are good, misunderstand or abuse other Church teachings and devotions.

Nonetheless, it's important not to continue walling off the practice of indulgences from both the clergy and the faithful. Instead, we need more teaching and discussion about them. We should not be avoiding them. They should be brought back into the open.

Currently, the structure for obtaining indulgences greatly reduces, if not nearly eliminates, game playing or rote performance of works to legitimately obtain indulgences. Should those things occur, no indulgence would be earned.

The reason for that is because one's frame of mind is so explicitly an integral part of each indulgence — not that such should not have been the case before, but now so much can be built around life's daily activities with a fuller spiritual desire to actually gain an indulgence.

In adhering to the current regulations, one can no longer obtain an indulgence haphazardly or in a meaningless way. Even if one thinks that they can unseriously do that, they won't secure the indulgence in the end.

Indulgences have always promoted prayer, especially for the Souls in Purgatory who need our prayers, but also for the need for penance for our own sins. Indulgences influenced many older people, growing up, to sincerely pray when they may not have otherwise done so. Today, properly obtained indulgences offer support not just for prayer, but as an aid to live our lives more fully in Christ and in our love for God.

How can anyone object to being encouraged to raise our minds in humble confidence to God in the performance of each daily activity? Can someone say that it is now too easy to satisfy the requirements to obtain a plenary indulgence? And, if people do still try to "play games," they would almost assuredly not be in the proper frame of mind to obtain the indulgence, possibly obtaining just a partial indulgence, though perhaps none at all.

When people fully understand what the Church has done for us in providing indulgences in their current form, this question should no longer be a concern.

QUESTION 2.

Q. I UNDERSTAND WHAT YOU ARE SAYING, BUT I STILL ENVISION PEOPLE OFFERING PIOUS INVOCATIONS ALL DAY LONG BEFORE EVERYTHING THEY DO. SURELY, THAT SORT OF THING CAN DETERIORATE INTO A MEANINGLESS ACTIVITY!

A. Of course, it can. But, at that point, there would be little doubt either that indulgences are no longer being gained, or that the person has actually become truly dedicated to the service of God.

In speaking again about Daily Life Indulgences (the first general grant or concession), it must be remembered that an integral part of the indulgence process is the raising of the mind in humble confidence to God, or in some other mode of positive spirituality. Such works must always be performed in proper frames of mind and heart and with a sincere spirit.

Regarding the First Grant, the *Manual of Indulgences* says:

"Owing to human weakness, such special acts are not frequent.

"*Should someone be devout and zealous enough to fill the day with such acts, he would justly merit, over and above the increase of grace, a fuller remission of punishment, and he can bring in his charity more abundant aid to the souls in purgatory.*"

QUESTIONS 3 AND 4

Q3. WHY DON'T WE HEAR ABOUT
INDULGENCES ANYMORE?
DOESN'T THAT MEAN THEY
REALLY AREN'T IMPORTANT FOR
US? Q4. ISN'T THIS LIKE MAKING A
DEAL WITH GOD?

Q UESTION 3.
Q. I HAVE HEARD ALMOST NOTHING
MENTIONED ABOUT INDULGENCES IN
RECENT DECADES. IF THEY REALLY HAVE ANY
IMPORTANCE AND MEANING, WOULDN'T THE BISH-
OPS, PRIESTS, AND RELIGIOUS TALK ABOUT THEM
MORE OFTEN? WOULDN'T THEY BE TAUGHT MORE
CONSISTENTLY BOTH IN AND OUT OF OUR
PAROCHIAL SCHOOLS AND IN ADULT RELIGIOUS
EDUCATION PROGRAMS TODAY?

A. Indulgences do have real importance and meaning. But
you bring attention to a real problem.

Bishops and the clergy themselves must learn again —
or perhaps for the first time — why indulgences are important and also about their proper use. More than that, many
clergy need to begin to personally use indulgences regularly
in their own lives. That is not only so as to gain remission

for the punishment due to their own sins, but also for the souls suffering in Purgatory.

They must then *teach* the importance and use of indulgences — and the regulations concerning them — to others. Such teaching should come from the pulpit on Sundays, as well as made an ongoing part of religious instruction, including that of our youngest Catholic children.

The proper use of indulgences can lead to the strengthening of our spiritual lives and draw each of us closer to God. They can help not only the Souls in Purgatory, but also ourselves.

QUESTION 4.
Q. ISN'T THIS LIKE MAKING A DEAL WITH GOD?

A. Obviously, it would be foolish and presumptuous for us to offer a deal to God.

On the other hand, throughout the long history that unfolds in the Bible, God has always offered "deals" to us. God told specific people, tribes, and nations that if they did something, He would do something else. God knows the outcome, but the choice was theirs — as it is ours today.

Take the story of Sodom and Gomorrah. Abraham asked God to spare the towns if fifty righteous men could be found. God agreed to Abraham's "deal" to spare the towns. But Abraham was not satisfied and bargained further with God to spare the town... if just ten righteous men could be found. Of course, God knew the result of a search for even ten righteous men, but He made what Abraham thought was a deal anyway.

Jesus also makes deals with us. Follow me and be saved,

He tells us. The deal is that if we follow Him, we will be saved. "Deals" where God is concerned are not new. He lets us use our free will to decide whether we will accept them or not.

In the case of indulgences, it is always God who makes the final decision whether or not to accept the merits of any indulgence we gain. If God Himself determines that a soul will remain in Purgatory until the final day of judgment on earth, it may not matter how many indulgences are obtained for that soul. In the end, it is up to God whether to apply an indulgence to any particular soul and to determine whether any indulgence has been properly earned. Of course, God does the same even outside of indulgences.

However, Jesus gave His Church the keys to the kingdom. So it would certainly appear likely that He would accept and grant the rewards earned by those who follow His Church's teachings and doctrines.

Perhaps it is like making a deal with God — but we must learn to trust in the power of prayer, in the Divine Mercy, and in Jesus Christ, the head of His Church on earth.

You must remember that indulgences make use of the satisfactions and graces won by Jesus and the saints which are a part of the treasury of the Church. Through the use of indulgences, those abundant merits and graces are dispensed by the Church in greater proportion for the remission of punishment due to sins. The practice of properly obtaining indulgences can also increase our spirituality. That, alone, can stand us in better stead with God.

The game has already been won by Jesus and we are still benefiting from His winnings.

This is a good deal that has been made with us.

QUESTIONS 5 AND 6

Q5. WHAT GIVES THE CATHOLIC
CHURCH THE RIGHT TO SAY
ANYTHING ABOUT CHANGING
OUR PUNISHMENT AFTER WE DIE?
Q6. I FIND INDULGENCES
MEANINGLESS AND WILL NEVER
USE THEM. WHAT DO YOU SAY
ABOUT THAT?

Q UESTION 5.
Q. WHAT GIVES THE CATHOLIC CHURCH
THE RIGHT TO SAY THAT PUNISHMENT DUE
AFTER DEATH IS NO LONGER DUE? DOESN'T GOD
ENTER INTO THIS SOMEWHERE?

A. God always has the right to determine whether or not an indulgence is earned and granted.

It might help you to again refer to the Parable of the Sorry Boy. Remember that it was the boy's *father* who assigned the punishment. But his *mother* was able to modify it. His mother trusted in her knowledge and love of the boy's father — and also in the love and mercy she knew that John's father has towards his son. In this situation, the boy's father had entrusted his guidance and authority to the boy's mother.

Nevertheless, had he wished, his father could still step in and require the punishment as originally given, regardless of the arrangements with the boy's mother. However, he is more likely to honor the judgement of his son's mother since he granted to her the authority in this situation.

Indulgences in the Catholic Church have a solid foundation in divine revelation as comes from the Apostles. They were discussed at the Council of Trent's 25th Session. A valuable and more complete discussion of this, with references, is found in the *Manual of Indulgences* itself.

QUESTION 6.

Q. IN SPITE OF EVERYTHING YOU'VE SAID — AND THE CHURCH'S OWN TEACHINGS WHICH I FINALLY READ IN THE *MANUAL OF INDULGENCES* — I STILL FIND THEM SILLY, CONFUSING, MEANINGLESS, AND WITHOUT FOUNDATION. I CAN'T ACCEPT THEM AND WILL NEVER USE THEM, EITHER FOR MYSELF OR FOR THE SOULS IN PURGATORY.

A. Then don't. God gave you free will just as He gave to the rest of us. Some people have more faith in God and His Church than do others. Rather than trying to persuade you further of the value of Church indulgences, I might instead suggest praying for an increase in both faith and love. You don't object to praying, do you?

But, even if you don't believe in the value of indulgences, what's it going to hurt to use them? Do you have an objection to lifting your mind to God on occasion during the day? Do an occasional few words such as *"All for you, Lord"* offend your sensibilities? Do you find reading Scripture or making a 30 minute visit to a church foolish and a waste of your time? Which specific actions do you object to that the

Church prescribes as part of the process of obtaining indulgences?

It is true that, even if you perform the actions prescribed by the Church, you will still not gain an indulgence since you do not have the intention to obtain one. But I don't think that is where the problem lies.

Could the real problem be that you are not living as both God and the Church teach us to do — regardless whether or not indulgences are involved?

Satan enjoys encouraging us to pick and choose what we want to believe, not only in regard to Church teachings, but even of the teachings and commandments of God. We find that guidance and direction both in Scripture and in many private revelations. After all, the less we do to maintain our presence before God, the more our Adversary succeeds.

QUESTIONS 7 AND 8

Q7. WHY DON'T OTHER PEOPLE
DEDICATE MORE OF THEIR
PRAYERS TO THE SOULS IN
PURGATORY? Q8. PLEASE EXPLAIN
THE CHURCH'S TEACHING ON
PURGATORY.

QUESTION 7.
Q. I HAVE ALWAYS DEDICATED ALL OF MY
PRAYERS TO THE SOULS IN PURGATORY. I
AM HAPPY TO LEARN MORE ABOUT THE CURRENT
REGULATIONS ON CHURCH INDULGENCES. I DON'T
UNDERSTAND WHY OTHER PEOPLE DON'T DEDI-
CATE ALL OF THEIR PRAYERS TO THE POOR SOULS.

A. It is gratifying to find people who place such importance
on prayers for the Souls in Purgatory. We gain intercessors
when we do. But you must remember that there are other
things to pray for which are also important, but to which
indulgences do not apply.

Prayers should also be offered for things such as:
personal peace in our lives and in the world; reparations
for the great injuries our sins have caused to the Sacred
Heart of Jesus and the Immaculate Heart of Mary; for
protection, strength, and wisdom for the Holy Father; for
faith, health, and protection of our clergy; for vocations

and a stronger support for them by the Church; for our own internal strength to fight the temptations of the devil; finding or a return to a life of commitment to God; and for the intentions of Our Lady — among countless other intentions.

Especially in these troubled times, it is important to pray for the conversion of sinners. Even without our prayers, the suffering Souls in Purgatory will eventually reach Heaven. But if people do not change their lives here on Earth, they will never see God.

Other intentions are indeed important. Even without indulgences, prayers are badly needed for the countless Souls in Purgatory who have no one to pray for them. All this is why it is important to pray without ceasing (1 Thessalonians 5:17).

As we have been reminded by Our Lady in recent years, people have forgotten that through the power of prayer and fasting, wars can be stopped and the laws of nature suspended.

QUESTION 8.

Q. I HAVE NEVER FULLY UNDERSTOOD THE CHURCH'S TEACHINGS ON PURGATORY. I DON'T KNOW ANY OTHER RELIGION THAT SUPPORTS THE TEACHINGS OF THE CATHOLIC CHURCH ABOUT PURGATORY.

A. The doctrine of Purgatory is understandable both from a point of logic, as well as what is alluded to in a verse in Scripture. That verse observes an expiatory sacrifice made for the dead after a battle:

"Therefore, he had this expiatory sacrifice offered for the dead so that they might be delivered from their sin" (2 Maccabees 12:46; New Catholic Bible).

An expiatory sacrifice refers to atonement for sins or guilt... "so that they might be delivered from their sin."

Nonetheless, there is no reason to pray for the dead if they are already with God in Heaven, nor is there a reason to pray for them if they are condemned to Hell. Why else, then, would prayers be offered?

There must, therefore, be an intermediate place where the dead referred to in this verse would be... waiting. They would be suffering for their sins and waiting to be *"...delivered from their sin."*

Most people assume that only people who are fully cleansed from their sins are able to enter Heaven. Those with unforgiven sins, or sins for which some punishment is necessary, would be in a place where the cleansing/punishment for those sins would take place before finally being taken into Heaven. If their sin is too serious, they may be condemned to Hell and not have an opportunity to be taken to Heaven at all. Rationally, therefore, there must be a place of cleansing.

2 Maccabees suggests that we can offer sacrifices/prayers/works to make up for some or all of the punishment due for sins for those waiting and suffering in Purgatory. But, again, even without its mention in Scripture, a rational amount of critical thinking can only lead us to the logical existence of Purgatory.

Additionally, but importantly, various apparitions over the years — including Our Lady's appearances in Medjugorje — have specifically asked that we pray for the Souls in Purgatory. There have been multiple times in multiple apparitions where we have been asked to pray for the Poor Souls in Purgatory.

In Question 25, you will hear of one report of apparitions many years ago by a number of souls in Purgatory — as they asked for help for themselves.

A few other churches also discuss a place of waiting, a place short of Heaven. They do not use the same terminology as Catholicism and often try to distance themselves from Catholic teachings. But some of those can have a similar feel to the doctrine of Purgatory as found most clearly and authoritatively in Catholicism.

You can find more information on the Catholic doctrine of Purgatory in various books, including the Catechism of the Catholic Church. You might also want to discuss it with a Catholic priest or other knowledgeable clergyman.

QUESTION 9 AND 10

Q9. ARE PARTIAL INDULGENCES
ONLY FOR SINS THAT HAVE BEEN
FORGIVEN? Q10. WHY IS GOING TO
CONFESSION FREQUENTLY
RECOMMENDED REGARDLESS OF
INDULGENCES?

Q*UESTION 9.*
Q. ARE PARTIAL INDULGENCES, IN
PARTICULAR, ONLY FOR THOSE SINS THAT
HAVE BEEN FORGIVEN?

A. Yes — and that is another good reason to get to
confession often. Even without concerns about indulgences,
monthly confession is often recommended.

That being the case, it would appear that, in many cases,
souls may still have to spend time in Purgatory to atone for
sins that were not forgiven prior to their death.

Although there is an alternative to a proper confession
when someone displays *perfect contrition* — not necessarily a
sure thing — the proper reception of the Sacrament of
Penance (Reconciliation; Confession) with sincere contrition remains the surest way to obtain forgiveness for our
sins.

The *Manual of Indulgences* states that *"An indulgence is a
remission before God of the temporal punishment for sins, <u>whose</u>*

guilt is forgiven..." [emphasis added]. The *Manual* also refers to performing an indulgenced action for a partial indulgence "...*with at least inward contrition.*"

QUESTION 10.

Q. SO SHOULD I GO TO CONFESSION EVERY TWO WEEKS IN ORDER TO OBTAIN A DAILY PLENARY INDULGENCE? IT SOUNDS AS THOUGH YOU'RE ALSO SUGGESTING THAT EVEN PEOPLE WHO ARE NOT OBTAINING PLENARY INDULGENCES SHOULD GO TO CONFESSION AT LEAST MONTHLY. IS THAT RIGHT?

A. First, you must not assume that simply by going to confession every two weeks you will be able to obtain daily plenary indulgences. For most people, obtaining a plenary indulgence each day is not easy to do. *The Manual of Indulgences* itself is well aware of our "human weakness." It is also aware that to *properly* obtain plenary indulgences on a consistent basis would require a devotion and zealousness not found in most people.

In the distant past, confession had been recommended as little as once during one's lifetime. Certainly there are those who may have neither serious nor lesser sins to confess. One should not make a confession of a frivolous nature. A lack of seriousness does not support the dignity of the sacrament. However, even venial sins should be confessed with contrition and seriousness. Some simply need the grace of confession as an aid in their daily living in God.

In addition, with the increasingly serious shortage of priests in many places, the sacrament may become even less available than it has been. That does not mean that confession for venial or repeated sins is not important. It is. The grace for confession is important in all situations as we work to improve our spiritual strength and reduce our sinfulness.

There have been increasingly strong recommendations to receive the sacrament on a monthly basis. Even Our Lady has suggested that. Indeed, certain devotions, such as the First Saturday devotion, call for monthly confession. People really should try to get back in the habit of monthly confession.

Of course, one should always go to confession when a serious sin is involved. And the sacrament must be treated with the respect due to all of the sacraments. But the preparation of mind and heart necessary for a meaningful confession and for the grace obtained make frequent confession especially valuable. Even should you feel a proper contrition may not be present, you might obtain important insights and help by talking about it to a priest.

An author's aside on confession follows.

AN AUTHOR'S ASIDE: CONFESSION

For many years now, the Sacrament of Penance has not been adequately promoted in many places. The clergy, in particular, must actively promote this important and healing sacrament. The prophets didn't wait for people to come to them to seek God's will. They spread God's messages even to people who didn't want to hear about them. They didn't assume that, since everyone had heard what God wanted at sometime in their life, they didn't need to hear about it again.

All clergy must learn to sell the importance of this sacrament, not just to the faithful, but perhaps even to themselves. It's unfortunate that a few priests have seemed to become apathetic, even bothered about having to administer such a vital sacrament.

Robust attendance at confession can be a sign of a successful priest — and of healthy souls.

Confessions scheduled for Saturday afternoons, for example, are fine, but only if enough of the faithful take advantage of them. But if they are not well-attended, they should be rescheduled or additional opportunities added during the week.

Long lines are now only rarely seen even at some larger parishes. Indeed, in many places, priests can find the short time set aside for weekly confessions to be a good time to catch up on their reading.

How can priests justify being comfortable after witnessing a sparsely-attended Holy Day of Obligation pass, only to see little or no increase in the already small numbers of attendees at the next scheduled time for confession?

Priests often think that the faithful know what they are supposed to do and that it's their responsibility to get to confession, not the priest's to drag them there.

But that assumption is wrong. Today, the faithful often do *not* know about these things.

For many decades, catechesis in most places, for both children and adults, has been woefully inadequate. The clergy must reach out and teach the basics of Catholicism, as well as additional doctrine they assume Catholics know about, but really don't.

Priests are a vital link to God and to the inner peace that God provides to the penitent through the Sacrament of Penance. Time must again be taken to bring the peace, love, counseling, and reassurance of the sacrament to the faithful of the Church. People need the strength and peace that should come to them from God through the priest.

Token penances, such as one Our Father or three Hail Marys for serious sins, minimize the seriousness of sin for many penitents. Such can reduce the perceived power and importance of the sacrament. After all, what is the purpose for penance? The Church has remained clear on its continued importance for us.

On the other hand, more robust penances might not be completed, potentially adding a new failing for the penitent.

Parishes need to reschedule confessions to the days and times when more people are likely to attend. Although not always possible, providing confessions, even if just occasionally, before or after Sunday Masses might bring many more people back to the Eucharist and certainly reduce the number of sacrilegious receptions of the Sacrament.

Periodic or regular weekday evenings can be a viable scheduling option in some parishes. *"By appointment"* alone, without additional regularly scheduled times, at least weekly, is usually not a good option. Its lack of privacy can also discourage many people from calling for an "appointment."

Whenever scheduled, confession should be at times and on days that the faithful will attend — and not on unchanging scantily-attended days and times out of past habit and tradition. Further, the sacrament should regularly be promoted from the pulpit — not merely once or twice each year. (Yes, it's all much more work for priests to do this.)

Frequent confession should do more than simply keep us aware of our own sinfulness and that God's forgiveness is available to us. The sacrament should put within us the desire and grace to be better. It should be a help in overcoming another serious disorder about which Scripture expresses disdain: apathy (Revelation 3:15, 16).

And spiritual apathy and indifference are currently rampant.

As part of the Catholic community and the Body of Christ, people must again experience the fulfillment and peace of reconciliation with God — and with themselves.

This sacrament gives us the grace to yet again make a running start at living our lives with the constant awareness of God's power, presence, and forgiveness. We should all become more welcoming of this powerful, loving — and necessary — sacrament.

QUESTION 11 – 14

Q11. WHAT DOES IT MEAN TO BE A SUBJECT OF THE ONE GRANTING AN INDULGENCE? Q12. ARE THERE OTHER INDULGENCES NOT LISTED IN THE MANUAL OF INDULGENCES? Q13. ARE INDULGENCES THE ONLY WAY TO HELP OURSELVES AND THE SOULS IN PURGATORY? Q14. IS THERE A DAILY LIMIT ON GAINING PARTIAL INDULGENCES?

QUESTION 11.

Q. ONE OF THE PREREQUISITES IN ORDER FOR A PERSON TO BE CAPABLE OF OBTAINING AN INDULGENCE IS BEING A SUBJECT OF THE ONE GRANTING AN INDULGENCE. DOESN'T THAT MERELY MEAN THAT ONE MUST BE A CATHOLIC AND THEREBY A SUBJECT OF THE POPE? ISN'T THAT WHAT IT MEANS?

A. It is more than just that. In addition to the indulgences enumerated in the *Manual of Indulgences,* the Church allows diocesan bishops, and others specifically mentioned, to grant indulgences to persons under their jurisdiction. Some of those indulgences can relate to things specifically in their dioceses.

For example, a diocesan bishop might give a papal blessing, to which a plenary indulgence is attached, three times a year on solemn feasts of their own choosing. There are also other opportunities for bishops to provide indulgences to the faithful. However, in order to obtain these indulgences, a person must be a subject of that bishop. Members of the bishop's diocese would, of course, be subject to the bishop.

Unfortunately, it often appears that diocesan bishops are either unaware of, or unsupportive of this privilege. Most bishops rarely, if ever, exercise this right. When it is exercised, the faithful are rarely made aware of these additional opportunities to obtain indulgences — or, even more fundamentally, made aware of what indulgences even are.

QUESTION 12.

Q. ARE THERE OTHER APPROVED INDULGENCES NOT LISTED IN THE *MANUAL OF INDULGENCES?*

A. Religious orders, pious associations of the faithful, and other groups can have indulgences specifically applicable to them. Members of those groups should look into indulgences, or changes to them, which specifically apply to them. In addition, the Apostolic See periodically offers what are sometimes just one-time indulgences.

QUESTION 13.

Q. ARE INDULGENCES THE ONLY WAY TO HELP OURSELVES AND THE SOULS IN PURGATORY?

· · ·

A. We should remember that *"the departed can be assisted, not only by means of indulgences, but also by other manifold ways: prayers, penitential acts, works of charity, almsgiving, and especially by the celebration of the Mass."* (*Enchiridion of Indulgences, 1968, English: 1969.*)

Prayers and our other good works can certainly be offered for the Souls in Purgatory — and for ourselves — even if we don't choose to enrich them with indulgences. However, using indulgences makes such prayers and works even more valuable. We can also make others aware of the availability of Church indulgences and the special opportunities they provide to further help both ourselves and the Souls in Purgatory.

Keep in mind that indulgences are offered by the Church in order to assist us in obtaining the remission of punishment due to sin. However, this in no way means that God Himself cannot or does not forgive such punishment in other ways through His Divine Mercy.

QUESTION 14.

Q. I UNDERSTAND THAT ONLY ONE PLENARY INDULGENCE CAN BE OBTAINED PER DAY, WITH THE ONE EXCEPTION BEING AT THE MOMENT OF DEATH. IS THERE ALSO A LIMIT ON GAINING PARTIAL INDULGENCES?

A. No, there is no such limit. Unless otherwise indicated, partial indulgences may be obtained often throughout the day.

QUESTIONS 15 – 18

Q15. CAN VISITS TO CHURCHES, WHEN REQUIRED TO GAIN CERTAIN INDULGENCES, BE MADE THE EVENING BEFORE? Q16. CAN I GET AN INDULGENCE FOR DOING THE PENANCE GIVEN TO ME IN CONFESSION? Q17. DOES AN INDULGENCE ATTACHED TO THE USE OF AN ARTICLE OF DEVOTION EVER STOP? Q18. DO I HAVE TO SAY INDULGENCED PRAYERS OUT LOUD?

QUESTION 15.

Q. THE OBLIGATION TO ATTEND MASS ON SUNDAYS AND ON HOLY DAYS OF OBLIGATION MAY BE SATISFIED BY ATTENDING DESIGNATED MASSES THE EVENING BEFORE. CAN A VISIT TO CHURCHES, WHEN REQUIRED TO GAIN AN INDULGENCE ON A PARTICULAR DAY, ALSO BE MADE THE EVENING BEFORE?

A. Such visits may be made *"...from noon of the preceding day until midnight of the particular day."*

QUESTION 16.

Q. CAN I GET AN INDULGENCE FOR DOING THE PENANCE GIVEN TO ME IN CONFESSION?

A. One cannot get an indulgence by doing something that is required by "law or precept," [21§1] unless expressly stated to the contrary. However, a work or prayer that satisfies the penance assigned by a priest during confession, may gain, in addition, an indulgence — but only if such required work or prayer (as part of the penance) would normally be indulgenced [21§2] — and, naturally, under the usual conditions, including the intent to obtain the indulgence.

QUESTION 17.
Q. DOES AN INDULGENCE ATTACHED TO THE USE OF AN ARTICLE OF DEVOTION EVER STOP?

A. Such indulgences cease "only *if the article is destroyed or sold.*" [16§2]

Crucifixes, crosses, rosaries, scapulars, and medals are the only articles of devotion to which an indulgence can be attached as listed in the *Manual of Indulgences.*[1] [15]

In addition, there is no difference between one rosary and another, or for a different sacred article, other than the requirement for gaining the plenary indulgence obtainable on the Unfortunately, it often appears that diocesan bishops

---

1.   Note that, according to the *Enchiridion of Indulgences (1968, English: 1969),* these articles are simply *"an occasion for gaining indulgences, insofar as they serve as a reminder and a help to perform the pious work and to perform the pious work more readily."*

are either unaware of, or unsupportive of this privilege. Most bishops rarely, if ever, exercise this right.

As noted before, even when it is exercised, the faithful are rarely made aware of these additional opportunities to obtain indulgences — or, even more fundamentally, made aware of what indulgences even are.

On that day, the faithful making prayerful use of an article blessed by the Supreme Pontiff or a bishop would be granted a plenary indulgence (under the usual conditions). [Norm N17 adds the requirement to make any legitimate profession of faith.]

However, the prayerful use of such an article properly blessed by a priest or a deacon would be granted a partial indulgence. [14]

QUESTION 18.

Q. IN ORDER TO GAIN AN INDULGENCE THAT IS ATTACHED TO A PRAYER, DO I HAVE TO SAY THE PRAYER OUT LOUD?

A. Not necessarily. The prayer may be said alternately with a companion, or even just followed mentally while someone else says it. The practice in many churches of saying the Rosary before or after a Daily or Sunday Mass is a good opportunity to gain a plenary indulgence — assuming the other requirements for the indulgence are met.

Too often, they are not.

Devout time spent in mental prayer is specifically mentioned as being enriched with a partial indulgence — if someone has the proper disposition and intention as required for all partial indulgences. [15]

QUESTION 19 – 22

Q19. CAN PEOPLE WHO ARE
SERIOUSLY PHYSICALLY IMPAIRED
GET INDULGENCES? Q20. IF I AM IN
DANGER OF DEATH, HOW CAN I
FULFILL THE CONDITIONS FOR A
PLENARY INDULGENCE IF A PRIEST
IS NOT AVAILABLE? Q21. ARE SOME
INDULGENCES SPECIFICALLY FOR
THE DEAD, AND CANNOT BE
APPLIED FOR THE REMISSION OF
THE PUNISHMENT DUE FOR OUR
OWN SINS? Q22. WHAT IS AN
ORATORY?

QUESTION 19.

Q. WHAT IF SOMEONE IS PHYSICALLY UNABLE TO COMPLETE ALL THE CONDITIONS REQUIRED TO GAIN AN INDULGENCE?

A. The Church makes provisions for people who are legitimately impeded from completing the requirements necessary to gain an indulgence.

Confessors (those who know and support indulgences; today many don't and might not be of help) have the power to commute the required conditions or the prescribed work itself for someone who, *"because of a legitimate impediment,"* finds it impossible to perform the prescribed work. [Norm24]

Those who have such impediments and who wish to gain indulgences are encouraged to talk to their confessor. (Also refer to the *Manual of Indulgences.*)

Additionally, local ordinaries (normally a bishop) can grant to the faithful under their jurisdiction permission to obtain a plenary indulgence without confession or communion if they live in places where it is very difficult or impossible to go to confession or receive communion.

However, such faithful must *"have contrition for their sins and have the intention of receiving these Sacraments as soon as possible."* [Norm25]

In the case of the deaf and dumb, indulgences attached to public prayers may be gained if *"they devoutly raise their mind and affections to God"* while others are praying in the same place.

For private prayers, it is enough that they recite the prayers mentally or with signs, or if they merely read them without pronouncing the words. [Norm26]

QUESTION 20.

Q. IF I WANTED TO GAIN A PLENARY INDULGENCE FOR MYSELF WHEN I AM IN DANGER OF DYING, HOW WOULD I BE ABLE TO FULFILL ALL OF THE NECESSARY CONDITIONS IF A PRIEST IS NOT AVAILABLE?

A. In her concern for us, the Church has permitted a special plenary indulgence at the moment of death. For the faithful to obtain this, they must be in danger of death, *"properly disposed and have been in the habit of reciting some prayers during their lifetime."* The use of a crucifix or cross to gain this indulgence is encouraged, though apparently not required.

The condition that the person has been in the habit of reciting some prayers during their lifetime fulfills the three usual conditions of confession, communion, and prayers for the Holy Father's intentions only for purposes of obtaining this indulgence.

The *Manual of Indulgences* does not define what it means to be "in the *habit*" of saying prayers, as distinct from simply saying prayers once in a while, or even rarely.

An effort to pray regularly, *habitually*, is important for our spiritual health even beyond this requirement at the point of death.

But being *"in the habit of reciting some prayers during their lifetime"* is explicitly required for this important indulgence.

This is the only time a plenary indulgence can be gained even if another one had been obtained on the same day.

This specific plenary indulgence is especially for those who cannot be assisted by a priest to bring them the sacraments and impart the Apostolic Blessing with its plenary indulgence. [12]

It is *specifically required* that this be included in catechetical instruction of the faithful and that the faithful *be frequently reminded* of it. [12§5]

Unfortunately, catechetical instruction today, especially in the U.S., is commonly very poor. The requirement of a reminder is among too many other foundational teachings of Catholicism which are often not even taught at all. In the case here, it is almost never included.

And frequent reminders? That is so rare as to again allow us to say that it all but never happens.

The responsibility for this failure does not rest with the faithful.

QUESTION 21.

Q. SOMEONE TOLD ME THAT SOME INDUL-
GENCES ARE SPECIFICALLY INTENDED FOR THE
DEAD AND THAT THEY CANNOT BE APPLIED FOR
THE REMISSION OF OUR OWN PUNISHMENT. IS
THAT TRUE?

A. Yes, it is. Although all indulgences may be applied to the
dead, some indulgences are exclusively for the dead.

For example, and among others, devoutly visiting a
cemetery and praying for the dead — even if only mentally
— may obtain for them a plenary indulgence on any and
each day from November 1st to the 8th. Throughout the rest
of the year, a partial indulgence may be obtained. These
indulgences may only be applied to the Souls in Purgatory.
[29§1:1°]

Another plenary indulgence, only applicable to the
Souls in Purgatory, calls for a pious visit to a church or a
public or semi-private oratory on All Souls Day, generally
November 2nd. (This day may be moved by the local Ordinary to the Sunday before or after that date.) As with any
such visit, an Our Father and the Creed must be said.
[29§1:2°]

QUESTION 22.

Q. THE *MANUAL OF INDULGENCES* MENTIONS
"ORATORIES" SEVERAL TIMES ESPECIALLY WHEN
TALKING ABOUT INDULGENCES REQUIRING VISITS
TO CHURCHES. WHAT IS AN ORATORY?

. . .

A. An oratory is a small chapel which may be part of the facilities for a religious order, a retreat house, school, or some other place. They are generally primarily used for private prayer, although Masses can also be said in them. Some are public, while others are semi-private and are just meant for use by a particular group of people.

QUESTION 23 – 24

Q23. CAN YOU GIVE ME ANOTHER
EXAMPLE OF SOMETHING LIKE AN
INDULGENCE IN SOCIETY TODAY?
Q24. ISN'T THERE SOME FLEXIBILITY
IN THE REQUIREMENTS FOR
OBTAINING INDULGENCES?

QUESTION 23.
Q. CAN YOU GIVE ME ANOTHER EXAMPLE OF SOMETHING THAT IS SIMILAR TO AN INDULGENCE IN SOCIETY TODAY?

A. All examples and analogies fall theologically short. However, another example of something like (but different from) an indulgence in society today might be the case of a prisoner released early due to good behavior. This form of something potentially comparable to a "partial indulgence" rewards the kind of ongoing behavior that prisoners are hoped to continue upon their release.

Here, again, the people offering the good-behavior indulgence (not a real indulgence) — gaining an early release — are not likely to be the same people who originally assigned the punishment. A court of law originally sentenced the prisoner, but the authority to release the prisoner early can shift to the prison, parole system, or to someone else.

If, in addition to consistently good behavior, a prisoner were to perform some heroically good act — perhaps saving the lives of a number of guards, visitors, or other prisoners at great risk to himself — a merciful governor, upon the recommendation of others, could grant a full pardon (a plenary indulgence).

The efforts of outsiders to work for the prisoner's release here might be partly comparable to our prayers for a soul in Purgatory.

Note that such prisoner "indulgences" cannot be applied to people who have committed a crime (sin), but have not yet been found guilty in court for it (~confession with an assigned penance) — nor accepted responsibility and, hopefully, also shown proper contrition for their crime. Such contrition might — but also might not — modify the punishment assigned by the judge.

Our sins must first be forgiven before we can gain indulgences for the punishment due for them.

Unlike what many people think, penances assigned in confession do not necessarily equate to the entire punishment due for confessed and forgiven sins. Guilt may be forgiven, but penances — especially in more recent times — are often token penances which likely do not fully make up for the punishment due for those sins. This is why additional penance and fasting to atone for our sins can be important.

Non-Catholics believe that Christ dying for our sins was enough, that He made up for everything due for our sins. But, scripturally, that is not the case. We can still owe punishment due for our sins.

QUESTION 24.

Q. I WAS TALKING TO OUR PASTOR ABOUT INDUL-GENCES. HE SAID THAT I COULD GET A PLENARY INDULGENCE FOR A TWO OR TWO AND A HALF DAY RETREAT EVEN THOUGH THE *MANUAL OF INDUL-GENCES* SAYS THAT ONE MUST SPEND *"AT LEAST THREE ENTIRE DAYS IN THE SPIRITUAL EXERCISES OF A RETREAT"* (emphasis added).

FEW RETREATS TODAY ENCOMPASS *"THREE ENTIRE DAYS,"* ESPECIALLY THOSE HELD ON WEEKENDS.

HE SAID THAT THE CHURCH ISN'T CONCERNED WITH THAT KIND OF STRICT REQUIREMENT. IT IS THE INTENT AND DISPOSITION OF THE PERSON GAINING THE INDULGENCE THAT REALLY MATTERS.

HE SEEMED TO SAY THAT THE *MANUAL OF INDUL-GENCES* JUST CONTAINS GENERAL GUIDELINES WHICH THE SPIRIT AND DISPOSITION OF AN INDI-VIDUAL CAN USE TO GUIDE HIM.

A. Unless he was providing a dispensation for a serious and legitimate disability you might have (as mentioned earlier and as permitted by the regulations), your pastor was likely not correct.

In part due to abuses of the past, as well as confusion regarding indulgences over the years, the Church has been very sensitive in developing the regulations. It does not wish to permit abuses of the indulgence process to occur again. Therefore, the current regulations are not guidelines. They are specifically formulated regulations by which the clergy and faithful are to abide. Where flexibility might exist, the *Manual of Indulgences* specifies it.

However, one should also take into account possible translation errors — a problem in the past — with some common sense, to assist in a careful application of the contents of the *Manual,* especially regarding the wording of some of the prayers.

When in doubt, the regulations and writings in the *Manual of Indulgences* control.

Gaining indulgences, especially plenary indulgences, are not necessarily easy. Obtaining satisfaction for sin is not a frivolous activity. Nonetheless, for someone with the proper disposition and intent, there are many opportunities to gain indulgences.

On the way, we can develop spiritual self-discipline and a greater awareness of God's presence in our lives.

The General Grants for partial indulgences permit an almost unlimited range of actions to be indulgenced – if one has the proper intent and frame of heart. It is primarily in working to gain plenary indulgences that one must be especially careful to understand and follow the current regulations promulgated by the Church.

Of course, we can still obtain satisfaction for sins through prayers, fasting, and good works, even without the special enrichment of indulgences.

Refer directly to the current *Manual of Indulgences* to know the specific actions and prayers prescribed by the Church so as to obtain indulgences. As has been repeatedly said, increasing our spiritual self-discipline and instilling a healthy spirituality in our daily lives — benefits which are beyond the indulgences themselves — are part of our reward.

· · ·

[At the time of this writing, obtaining a current copy of the *Manual of Indulgences* is far more difficult than it has been in the past. Hopefully, that will have changed by the time you read this book.]

QUESTION 25

Q25. A BOOK ABOUT APPARITIONS
OF THE POOR SOULS SEEMS TO
DISPUTE WHAT YOU ARE SAYING.
WHAT'S THE STORY?

Question 25.

Q. A BOOK THAT I READ — *My Discourse
With Poor Souls* — TALKED ABOUT SOMEONE IN
EUROPE WHO REPORTED VARIOUS SOULS IN PURGA-
TORY APPEARING TO HER. THE SOULS ASKED FOR HELP.
THEY TOLD HER VARIOUS THINGS INCLUDING THAT,
WHEREAS PLENARY INDULGENCES MAY RELIEVE SOME
SUFFERING, THEY MIGHT NOT ELIMINATE
PUNISHMENT.

ANOTHER SOUL WAS ASKED WHETHER HE
WANTED MASSES OFFERED. THE SOUL RESPONDED,
"I CANNOT SHARE IN WHAT I DID NOT BELIEVE IN."

A NUN IN PURGATORY REPORTEDLY SAID THAT
VERY FEW PEOPLE CAN ACTUALLY GAIN A PLENARY
INDULGENCE SINCE IT *"REQUIRES A SPECIAL CONDI-
TION OF THE HEART AND WILL WHICH IS RARE, AND
MORE RARE THAN ONE GENERALLY BELIEVES."*

THE BOOK GOES ON TO SAY THAT SOULS WHO
HAD NOTHING TO DO WITH INDULGENCES DURING

THEIR LIVES ON EARTH *"CAN RARELY BENEFIT FROM A PLENARY INDULGENCE, ONLY PERHAPS PARTIALLY."*

DOESN'T ALL OF THIS SEEM TO INDICATE THAT PLENARY INDULGENCES, AND PERHAPS EVEN THE MASS ITSELF, WILL NOT NECESSARILY RELEASE SOULS FROM PURGATORY AS THE CHURCH TELLS US?

A. As has already been said, the final decision as to whether or not an indulgence is applied to a soul, and to what degree, is in the hands of the justice and mercy of God. Yet, even within the book that you reference, it is apparent that the Mass and the process of indulgences have the potential to help the Souls in Purgatory.

For example, even if, as some souls appear to say in this question, they cannot fully benefit from an actual indulgence, they can benefit from the underlying prayers and actions, specifically offered up for the souls, which are required to obtain the indulgence in the first place.

Nonetheless, it is indeed true that it is not easy to get a plenary indulgence for the precise reason as stated in your question. It *"requires a special condition of the heart and will which is rare."*

When we spoke of plenary indulgences earlier, we heard that we must have no attachment to sin, even venial sin — something that isn't easy for most people, a requirement about which most aren't even fully aware.

We are also told that we must have a contrite heart. We must pray *"... 'out of the depths' of a humble and contrite heart,"* (Catechism of the Catholic Church, paragraph 2559).

Indulgences always involve a form of prayer for which our heart must have the right disposition — a humble and contrite heart. The growth of spirituality in our lives as we work to gain indulgences, regardless of the special benefits of the indulgences themselves, is what makes this process so valuable.

However, the level of true interior effort for a plenary indulgence is indeed such that obtaining one is *"more rare than one generally believes."* The process requires a self-discipline of body and spirit. After a time of regular and serious attention to the indulgence process, one can cultivate an ongoing habit of a new spirituality and a new closeness to God. That certainly sets us up to gain future plenary indulgences.

But it isn't always easy.

That is why a proper preparation, especially in regard to plenary indulgences, is so important. One of the souls in the book importantly says that we should *"sacrifice our will"* for God's will.

However, don't be discouraged or give up! The Church, buoyed by the many extraordinary graces obtained by Jesus and the saints, supports and encourages our efforts!

And remember that there are also other ways to help, not only the Souls in Purgatory, but ourselves, through contrition and penance even without indulgences.

Also remember that, despite its most recent copyright date, the information concerning indulgences in the book you reference, and the purported apparitions described, are pre-Vatican II — a time prior to the current regulations.

Both private revelations and what we hear even in some of Our Lady's recent apparitions show an ongoing consistency of revelation and concern regarding the Poor Souls which we should not ignore. Praying for them just one time truly isn't enough.

Regarding the book, *My Discourse With Poor Souls*,[1] it is a book which is very difficult to find at the time of this writing. Nonetheless, it is a worthwhile book to help us to understand what the Souls in Purgatory are going through, why they need our help, and what we can do to help them.

Should it become available or can be found, it is recommended by the author.

❧

As we come to the end, let me suggest that, in order to address concerns the Poor Souls raise in this private revelation, and so that you yourself might be a bit more comfortable that those suffering in Purgatory will benefit from your efforts, you can pray directly to God for them without the use of either indulgences or the Mass.

Pray that their suffering be eased and that they be brought to Heaven more quickly.

Such direct help for them can include both prayers and offering life's struggles and sacrifices up for them. While not as rich in merits and graces as are offering indulgences and the Mass, the Souls in Purgatory will benefit greatly nonetheless.

Pray especially for those whom you knew or loved in this lifetime, rather than just (unwisely) assume that everyone you knew has gone to Heaven. But also pray for the people you didn't know in this lifetime — and who may have no one else to pray for them...but you.

---

1. *My Discourse With Poor Souls*, by Eugenie Von Der Leyen. Translated by Elizabeth Cattana. First published in German. Copyright 1979 by Christiana-Verlag, Stein am Rhein, Switzerland. English translation published by: The Franciscan Minims of the Perpetual Help of Mary, The House of Atonement; Mexico.

Although it is neither necessary nor healthy to obsess about this at every moment, the bottom line is to pray for the Souls in Purgatory as often as possible. Just as you would not want to be forgotten, don't forget them.

Chapter Eight

ABOUT THE APPENDICES

The complete and authentic collection of prayers and pious works to which the Apostolic See has attached indulgences is found in the *Manual of Indulgences* which is, at the time of this writing, in its 4th edition. The reader should refer to the latest edition of the *Manual* for the most complete and authoritative information on indulgenced prayers and works, as well as for the up-to-date requirements and procedures.

However, so that the reader might understand the nature and diversity of those prayers and works, as well as to encourage the reading of the *Manual of Indulgences* itself, examples or summaries of indulgenced prayers and works are presented here.

〜

Appendix A

Examples of Pious Invocations;
Examples of Partial Indulgences;
Examples of Plenary Indulgences.

Appendix B
Calendar of Indulgences:
List of Specific Days;
Other Special Days;
Other Events.

APPENDIX A

PIOUS INVOCATIONS; PARTIAL INDULGENCES; PLENARY INDULGENCES

Pious Invocations

The following invocations and many others are suggested in the *Manual of Indulgences* and also in the older *Enchiridion of Indulgences*. However, the pious invocations presented in the *Manual* are just examples. The faithful are free to use others like them, as long as they are sincere and religiously appropriate.

Here is the explanation regarding pious invocations as found in the *Manual of Indulgences:*

> *"An invocation, in relation to an indulgence, is not to be considered a distinct work in itself, but rather is to be used as a complement to some other work by which the faithful raise their minds to God in humble trust, while carrying out their duties and bearing the hardships of life."*

(Especially see the First General Grant.)

～

MY GOD! •••• JESUS! •••• PRAISED BE JESUS CHRIST!
•••• ALL FOR YOU! •••• YOUR WILL BE DONE! ••••
HAVE MERCY ON ME! •••• HAIL MARY! •••• HEART
OF JESUS, IN YOU I TRUST! •••• O GOD, BE MERCIFUL
TO ME, A SINNER! •••• O LORD, INCREASE OUR
FAITH! •••• MY LORD AND MY GOD! •••• SPARE ME,
O LORD! •••• JESUS, MARY, JOSEPH! •••• HOLY
MOTHER OF GOD, EVER VIRGIN MARY, INTERCEDE
FOR US! •••• HOLY MARY, MOTHER OF GOD, PRAY
FOR US! •••• REMAIN WITH US, O LORD! •••• WE
ADORE YOU, O CHRIST, AND WE BLESS YOU,
BECAUSE BY YOUR HOLY CROSS YOU HAVE
REDEEMED THE WORLD!

Partial Indulgences

The following are samples of prayers enriched with partial
indulgences:

Anima Christi (Soul of Christ); The Magnificat; The Memo-
rare; Hail, Holy Queen (Salve Regina); Act of Contrition; Prayer
To One's Guardian Angel.

Any of six specific litanies including:

> *The Most Holy Name of Jesus; The Most Sacred Heart of Jesus;*
> *The Blessed Virgin Mary; St. Joseph; The Saints; and, The Most*
> *Precious Blood of Our Lord, Jesus Christ. ...as well as many*
> *other prayers.*

Approved forms of each prayer are found in the *Manual*
of Indulgences.

Also included are such simple prayers as:

AGIMUS TIBI GRATIAS (We Give You Thanks): *We give You thanks, Almighty God, for all your blessings: who live and reign forever and ever. Amen.*

ANGELE DEI (Angel Of God): *Angel of God, my guardian dear, to whom his love entrusts me here, enlighten and guard, rule and guide me. Amen.*

MARIA, MATER GRATIAE (Mary, Mother Of Grace): *Mary, Mother of grace and Mother of mercy, shield me from the enemy and receive me at the hour of my death.*

VENI, SANCTE SPIRITUS (Come, Holy Spirit): *Come, Holy Spirit, fill the hearts of your faithful and enkindle in them the fire of your love.*

~

Because of unintended translation errors or inconsistencies, as well as potential cultural differences — all of which can exist — it is likely not necessary to use the precise prayer wordings in the *Manual* if you are accustomed and prefer the same prayers with slightly different wordings, but which have the same meanings. The preciseness of prayers is generally different from the more precise requirements of most of the indulgenced actions.

~

SAMPLES OF PRESCRIBED WORKS FOR PARTIAL INDULGENCES

The following are samples of the countless works — when taking into account the General Grants — enriched with partial indulgences. The numbers preceding each indulgence refer to the numerical references of the additional concessions/grants[1] of indulgences in the *Manual*. Note that descriptions of the differences between plenary and partial indulgences are often described within the same grant.

However, unless stated otherwise, *all assume the usual requirements for an indulgence.*

~

(6) Granted to those who teach or study Christian doctrine.

(7§2-1°) A visit to the Blessed Sacrament for adoration.

(8§2-1°) Make an act of spiritual communion, using any duly approved pious formula.

(8§2-2°) Make an act of thanksgiving after Communion (e.g., Anima Christi; En ego, O bone et dulcissime Iesu). [Note that those prayers are just examples.]

(10) Taking part in a month of recollection.

(14) Devoutly using [specific] articles of devotion (crucifix or

---

1.   Note that the terms concessions and grants are used interchangeably here, even though there are nuanced differences in some contexts.

cross, rosary, scapular, or medal) properly blessed by any priest or deacon.

(15) Granted to the faithful who for their personal edification devoutly spend time in mental prayer.

(26§2-3°) Grace before and after meals: Devoutly offer some legitimately approved prayer of supplication and act of thanksgiving.

[Among others, the grant lists several prayers, as examples. They include: *Benedic, Domine: Bless us, O Lord, and these your gifts, which we are about to receive from your bounty, through Christ our Lord, Amen.* (From the *Book of Blessings*, #785.)]

(28§1) Devoutly signing themselves with the sign of the cross, using the customary words: *In the name of the Father, and of the Son and of the Holy Spirit. Amen.*

(30§1) Less than 30 minutes reading Sacred Scripture from a text approved by competent authority, as spiritual reading, and with the reverence due to the divine word.

Plenary Indulgences

The following are samples of prescribed works which can be used to obtain plenary indulgences. If, for a reasonable cause, a work cannot be completed, a partial indulgence can still be gained for the part completed if the work itself can fittingly be divided into separate parts, such as the Rosary.

The *Manual of Indulgences* lists *many* more opportunities for plenary indulgences than are listed below. As above, the specific grants below are just examples.

Some grants have multiple parts, all of which may not be included here. However, even if part is not included, the part(s) listed are expected to be enough to allow one to attain a plenary indulgence by using the included, prescribed work.

If available, please refer to the full, authentic listing of indulgences in the *Manual of Indulgences* for complete details and requirements for each plenary indulgence.

Note that for those wishing to obtain a plenary indulgence each day, the adoration of the Blessed Sacrament for at least 30 minutes, devout reading of Sacred Scripture for at least 30 minutes, the pious exercise of the Way of the Cross, and recitation of the Marian Rosary, as described below, may be especially accessible. Numbers at the front of each grant below refer to the grant/paragraph number in the *Manual*.

~

PAPAL BLESSING

(4) Devoutly receive a blessing imparted by the Supreme Pontiff to Rome and the World (*Urbi et Orbi*) ...[or by a bishop, but see the *Manual*] ... even if, because of reasonable circumstances, they are unable to be present physically at the sacred rite, provided that they follow it devoutly as it is broadcast live by television or radio.

. . .

EUCHARISTIC ADORATION AND PROCESSION

(7§1-1°) A visit to the Blessed Sacrament for adoration for at least a half hour;

(7§1-3°) Devoutly participate in a solemn Eucharistic procession, held inside or outside a church, of greatest importance on the Solemnity of the Body and Blood of Christ.

SPIRITUAL EXERCISES...

(10§1) Spend at least three entire days in the spiritual exercises of a retreat.

USE OF ARTICLES OF DEVOTION

(14§1) On the Solemnity of the Holy Apostles Peter and Paul, make prayerful use of an article of devotion, as defined by Norm 15, that has been blessed by the Supreme Pontiff or by any bishop, provided the faithful also make a Profession of Faith using any legitimate formula. [A blessing by a priest or deacon gains a partial indulgence.]

EUCHARISTIC ... COMMUNION

(8§1-1°)) Is present at the reception of Holy Communion for the first time or devoutly assist at the First Communion of others.

IN MEMORY OF THE PASSION AND DEATH OF THE LORD

(13§2) Personally make the pious Way of the Cross, or devoutly unite themselves to the Way of the Cross while it is being led by the Supreme Pontiff and broadcast live on television or radio.

(1) This must be done before the legitimately erected stations of the Way of the Cross.

(2) To erect the Way of the Cross, fourteen crosses are needed, to which it is customary to attach a picture or image representing the fourteen stations of Jerusalem.

(3) It is customary to use fourteen devotional readings, to which some vocal prayers are added. However, it is sufficient simply to meditate devoutly on the Lord's Passion and Death whereby reflection on the particular mysteries of the individual stations is not necessary.

(4) Progression from one station to another is required. However, if the pious exercise is made publicly, and moving station to station by all participants is not possible without inconvenience, it is sufficient that at least the one conducting the Way of the Cross progress from station to station, while the others remain in their place.

(5) Those who are legitimately impeded can acquire the same indulgence, if they spend some time, e.g., at least a quarter of an hour, in reading and meditating on the Passion and Death of Our Lord Jesus Christ.

[The grant goes on to offer equivalent pious exercises. It also addresses "some other pious exercise" for those in the Eastern Churches.]

PRAYERS TO THE BLESSED VIRGIN MARY

(17§1-1°) Devoutly recite the Marian rosary in a church or oratory, or in a family, a religious community, or an association of the faithful, and in general when several of the faithful gather for some honest purpose.

(17§1-2°) Devoutly join in the recitation of the rosary

while it is being recited by the Supreme Pontiff and broad-cast live by radio or television.

In other circumstances, the indulgence will be *partial*.

[See the *Manual of Indulgences* for more requirements for a plenary indulgence with the Rosary partially including that:

"Recitation of a third part of the rosary" (five decades, minimum, at the time of this writing), must be recited without interruption; devout meditation on the mysteries must be added to the vocal prayer; in a public recitation, the mysteries must be announced "in accord with approved local custom." [Note: Do bishops actually *approve* local customs?] In private recitation, it is sufficient simply to join meditation on the mysteries to the vocal prayer.

Note that the 4th Edition of the *Manual of Indulgences* is from 1999. In 1999, a full Rosary only consisted of the 15 mysteries of the Joyful, Sorrowful, and Glorious Mysteries.

However, in October 2002, Pope St. John Paul II promulgated the *Luminous Mysteries*. Although not included in the *Manual* at the time of this writing, it is quite likely that the *Luminous Mysteries* will be assumed to be, or will soon be designated as included with the other mysteries as part of a *full* Rosary.

In like way, it is possible that other mysteries will be considered for future inclusion in the full Rosary. For example, the *Loveful Mysteries,* or some other, might conceivably be added at a future time.[2]]

---

2. Especially see: *The Rosary: The New Loveful Mysteries, Meditation Beads, and More* (2022).

. . .

PROFESSION OF FAITH AND ACTS OF THE
THEOLOGICAL VIRTUES

(28§1) At the celebration of the Easter Vigil or on the
anniversary of their own Baptism, renew their baptismal
vows in any legitimately approved formula. [An aside: Note
that, for a plenary indulgence, this grant designates the
Easter *Vigil,* not Easter Sunday itself. Other renewals obtain
a *partial* indulgence.]

FOR THE FAITHFUL DEPARTED: *(Applicable only to the
Souls in Purgatory)*

(29§1-1°) On any and each day from November 1 to 8,
devoutly visit a cemetery and pray, if only mentally, for the
departed.

(29§1-2°) On All Souls' Day (or, according to the judgment of the ordinary, on the Sunday preceding or following
it, or on the Solemnity of All Saints), devoutly visit a church
or an oratory and recite an Our Father and the Creed.

READING OF SACRED SCRIPTURE

(30§1) Reading Sacred Scripture as spiritual reading,
from a text approved by competent authority and with the
reverence due to the divine word for at least half an hour. [If
the time is less, the indulgence will be partial.]

DIVINE MERCY SUNDAY

See Chapter 11 for the plenary indulgence on this day.

APPENDIX B
CALENDAR; SPECIAL DAYS; OTHER
EVENTS

Although most indulgences are not linked to any particular day, others are. Listed in this appendix are some days, dates, and events, mentioned in the *Manual of Indulgences* to which certain specific indulgences are linked. But they are not indulgenced by themselves.

The numbers after them refer to the numbered grants as listed in the *Manual* itself. Should you be able to obtain the *Manual*, you should refer to it for complete details as to the indulgences obtainable on any specific day or for other days and events.

Note that some of the specific days on which indulgences may be obtained may be changed by the local ordinary (the bishop), generally to the Sunday preceding or following the particular day.

Calendar of Indulgences

SPECIFIC DAYS (partial listing):

November 1st to 8th (on any and each day) (#29)

November 2nd: All Souls Day (#29)

Good Friday (#13)

Any Friday of Lent (#8)

Divine Mercy Sunday (Decree)

Solemnity of The Most Sacred Heart of Jesus (#3)

Solemnity of Our Lord Jesus Christ, King of the Universe(#2)

Solemnity of the Body and Blood of Christ (#7)

Prior to the Solemnity of Christmas (#22)

Prior to the Solemnity of Pentecost (#22)

Prior to the Solemnity of the Immaculate Conception (#22)

Solemnity of the Holy Apostles, Peter and Paul (#14; 33)

Memorial of any saint listed in the calendar (#21)

Mass of the Lord's Supper on Holy Thursday (#7)

First Day of the Year or the Solemnity of Pentecost (#26)

Last Day of the Year (#26)

August 2nd ("Portiuncula") (#33)

Easter Vigil (#28)

Easter Season (#17)

Other Special Days (partial listing):

Titular Feast (#33)

First Communion (#8)

First Mass of a Newly-Ordained Priest (#27)

For priests: celebrating Mass on the 25th, 50th, 60th, and 70th Anniversary of their Ordination (#27)

For bishops: Mass on the 25th, 40th, and 50th Anniversary of the Episcopal Ordination of a Bishop (#27)

Day of the consecration of a church or an altar (#33§1-6°)

Liturgical memorial of the founder of a church, oratory, or

institutes of consecrated life and societies of apostolic life (#33§1-7°)
Anniversary of one's Baptism (#28)

Other Events (partial listing):

Family consecration (#1)

Participate religiously in a Eucharistic procession (#7)

Eucharistic celebration at the close of a Eucharistic Congress (#7)

Spiritual exercises of a three-day retreat (#10)

At the point of death (#12)

Hear some of the sermons and are present during the time and solemn close of a mission (#16)

With attentiveness and devotion, assist at other occasions of the preaching of the Word of God (#16)

Universally designated day for certain religious intentions (#5)

Take part in a month of recollection (#10)

Visit to a Patriarchal Basilica, minor basilica, or the cathedral church of Rome (#33)

Visit to a properly established shrine (#33)

Diocesan Synod (#31)

Pastoral visit to a church (#32)

A stational church on its designated day (#33)

Blessing by the Supreme Pontiff to Rome and the World (Urbi et Orbi) (#4)

Week of Christian Unity (#11)

The Easter Season (#17)

Visit to a Christian cemetery (#29; #33)

Visit to an ancient Christian cemetery or catacomb (#33)

IMPRIMATURS AND OTHER THINGS

L et me begin by speaking for a moment about imprimaturs.

"The Church cannot live its mission if it silences voices through a broken imprimatur process."

Today, it does indeed appear to be a broken system. Certainly, we can easily say that it is not working in conformance with both the regulations and intent of the 1983 Code of Canon Law.

The imprimatur process is to determine whether a book conforms to Church morals and doctrine. That is its only tasking. But how can that possibly happen if a diocese will not review a book or, worse, if a bishop or other involved clergyman does not accept the very doctrine about which the book is written?

Added to that are books for which imprimaturs have been granted, but which contain clear doctrinal errors.

Even common localized forms of various devotional prayers, as used by both the faithful and the clergy, are not reviewed and approved by bishops as required by Canon Law.[1] That should be a very straightforward and simple process. Yet that, too, is ignored.

The current broken imprimatur system in much of America damages not only authors and publishers, but also the faithful. It has become a silent killer of an otherwise healthy Catholic publishing system in America — and likely beyond.

Penalizing authors, publishers and, by extension, the faithful, is not what the Holy See envisioned when it updated Canon Law in 1983.

I sincerely hope that many of the Church hierarchy will take a fresh and immediate look at their responsibilities — and then openly and unbiasedly embrace and fulfill them.

∾

Before ending, and while not intending to spend extensive time on them here, I take the liberty to briefly raise three additional concerns which too often occur within the responsibilities of the American hierarchy, generally the bishops, but also many priests:

(1) First is the ongoing failure to find and develop vocations to the priesthood. Unlike what we hear, there are many callings to vocations from God. But, by the actions of many current bishops, dioceses, and vocation directors in America, these nascent vocations are too often neither found nor harvested.

---

1. As just one of multiple examples of such failures, see commentary attached to Canon 997.

Even when they are, the actions of such vocation directors and others in a diocese can unnecessarily ensure the slow death of callings from God.

This failing too often lies with the Church itself. It is not necessarily from a lack of legitimate callings to religious vocations, including to the priesthood. God has called many people.

(2) Without spending the time needed to offer convincing details, I have recently noted that a number of American bishops appear to have inexplicably and arbitrarily publicly imposed what might appear to be a lifetime of punishment on certain people whom they judge from afar.

Such have seemed to be based on a changing political culture, combined with a changing social agenda in the U.S. Such actions appear to me to be a direct assault on the Church's doctrine of forgiveness — from Jesus Himself — as well as on the sacrament which facilitates such forgiveness. Such arbitrary condemnations have appeared to have unjustly hurt not only those who are publicly condemned, along with their life's work, but also have damaged the faithful and the broader Church itself.

(3) And one last thing.

Cardinal Prosper Grech of Malta had been invited to speak to the 115 Catholic cardinals who would eventually elect Pope Francis. He was 87 at the time. A *Catholic News Service* article of August 8, 2013, reported what Cardinal Grech said:

Too many Catholics ... do not know the teachings of the church;

> *not only does an ignorance and lack of care about Catholic doctrine reign, but also an ignorance of the basics of Christianity itself.*

Many surveys have backed up Cardinal Grech's observations.

Yet far too many bishops and parish priests oversee very poor OCIA programs — the Order of Christian Initiation for Adults — in which new Catholics are purportedly taught the fundamentals and doctrines of the Catholic Church and of Christianity itself.

Imagine an OCIA program sending new Catholics into the pews having never taught or even made the Sign of the Cross a single time during many weeks or months of "instruction." Countless other basic tenets of the Church are also ignored. Many such programs would feel just as much at home in an evangelical church as in Catholicism.

When Catholics don't know, don't understand, or don't accept their own Church's teachings, they are ripe for harvesting by other churches — and that happens on a regular basis.

One publication[2] called fallen-away Catholics the *"... second largest religious denomination in the United States."*

When Catholics understand and practice their faith, they are likely to stay Catholic. However, a weak foundation in understanding Catholicism continues to lead to the loss of countless Catholics.

This means that a great many of the faithful in the pews today do not know their own faith.

Fulton J. Sheen (1895–1979), a famous Catholic bishop (later titular archbishop), was widely known for his televi-

---

2. *Catholic Anchor,* April 2014, pg. 1.

sion evangelization programs in the 1950s. He was reportedly seen by 20 to 30 million viewers every week. Fulton Sheen famously once said:

There are not one hundred people in the United States who hate the Catholic Church, but there are millions who hate what they wrongly perceive the Catholic Church to be.

That is as true today as when his words were first spoken.

I am not alone in sounding this alarm. Over many years, others have concurred with Cardinal Grech, speaking and writing strongly to warn of the same thing. At all levels, catechesis in the Catholic Church needs a critical and urgent fix.[3]

Even and especially in our weaknesses, may the Lord strengthen and be with us all.

L.S. Scarpitta

2025

---

3. For more words on this, see an extensive digression in the 2022 book, *The Cartainos: Men of Passion • Men of Stone:* Digression: What Is It With the Catholic Church?

BIBLIOGRAPHY

Manual of Indulgences: Norms and Grants; translated from the 1999 fourth edition. 1st printing: 2006; English translation©2006, Liberia Editrice Vaticana; 5th printing: 2017. Licensee: United States Conference of Catholic Bishops.

Enchiridion of Indulgences (1969)
Catholic Book Publishing Company, New York

Encyclopedia of Theology: The Concise Sacramentum Mundi (1975); Edited by Karl Rahner. The Seabury Press, New York

Messages and Teachings of Mary at Medjugorje (1988) by Rene Laurentin and Rene Lejeune. The Riehle Foundation, Milford, Ohio

Modern Catholic Dictionary (1979)

New Catholic Encyclopedia (1967)
Catholic University of America

New Regulations on Indulgences (1970) by Father Winfrid Herbst, S.D.S.; Tan Book and Publishers, Inc., Rockford, Illinois

The Code of Canon Law: A Text and Commentary (1985)
Paulist Press, New Jersey

My Discourse With Poor Souls (1979), by Eugenie Von Der Leyen.
Translated by Elizabeth Cattana. First published in German.
Copyright 1979 by Christiana-Verlag, Stein am Rhein, Switzerland.
English translation published by: The Franciscan Minims of the Perpetual Help of Mary, The House of Atonement; Mexico.

The Raccolta: A Manual of Indulgences: Prayers and Devotions Enriched with Indulgences (1950; 1951), by Rev. Joseph P. Christopher, PhD; Rt. Rev. Charles E. Spence, M.A.; and Rt. Rev. John F. Rowan, D.D.

BIBLIOGRAPHY

OTHER BOOKS BY THE AUTHOR

Multi-Services Publishing Company

www.multiservicespublishing.com

BUYYOURBOOK.ONLINE

www.buyyourbook.com

Spiritual Reading:

Is God the Actual Entity of Love?

The Forgotten Treasure of Indulgences

The Rosary: The New Loveful Mysteries, Meditation Beads, and More

The Loveful Mysteries of the Rosary (booklet)

Secular Reading:

The Cartainos: Men of Passion, Men of Stone

Education Is Dead: Reflections on a Failed Public School System

Killers Are Fatherless: The Real Cause of School Shooters Serial Killers, and Gang Murders

www.ingramcontent.com/pod-product-compliance
Lightning Source LLC
LaVergne TN
LVHW011912080426
835508LV00007BA/501